Raising Knights & Princesses in a Dark Age

- - - - - - - - - - - - - - - - - - -

PRICELESS GEMS
FOR BRINGING UP
EXCEPTIONAL CHILDREN

- - - - - - - - - - - - - - - - - - -

Merry Christmas
2014
God Bless you
Rob Foster

Robert Foster

RAISING KNIGHTS & PRINCESSES IN A DARK AGE

Published by Summit University Media — www.SummitUniversityMedia.com

Cover design and content layout by Nathaniel Daeger.

Cover image is from God Speed! (1900) by Edmund Blair Leighton (1852-1922).

FIRST EDITION

ISBN 978-0-9881903-0-6

To my loving wife Carolyn,

and my four wonderful children,

Elizabeth, Timothy, Laura, and Adam.

CONTENTS

ACKNOWLEDGMENTS

First I would like to thank my wife and true love, Carolyn, for her commitment to me and to parenting and homeschooling our children. I would also like to thank our four wonderful children, Elizabeth, Timothy, Laura, and Adam, for making parenting such a joy.

Many friends supported the development of this book through the years. I would like to thank those who proofread many early manuscripts. Thanks to Paula Robb, Patty Stallings, Rachel Macdonald, Sherry Young, and Nate Daeger. Special thanks for the skilled service of my chief editor April Frazier and to Carol Berry as copy editor. I would also like to express my appreciation to Nate Daeger for cover design and layout.

Thanks also to my father and mother for giving me a loving example of parenting in my formative years. Also to my lifelong mentors Tim and Joanie Thomas, Larry and Nancy Schlager, Bill and Margaret Hossler, and Rick and Cathy Laymon.

As always, thanks to God the Father and Jesus Christ for salvation and providing the source of love and wisdom.

ABOUT THE AUTHOR

Dr. Robert Foster currently lives in Beijing, China. He holds degrees in education and business from Bethel College, Notre Dame, and Azusa Pacific University. He divides his time between strengthening families, developing emerging leaders, writing, and public speaking.

PREFACE

On a brisk winter's evening, my wife and four children bundled up to take the Beijing subway to visit friends. As usual, the subway was filled with late-night commuters and families returning from school activities in the city. Sitting next to us was a woman and her eight-year-old son, heading home after a full day of activities. We started a conversation with her and talked about our work. Her husband was involved in leadership, and I mentioned that I had authored a book on that topic. She immediately asked me if I had written anything on parenting, saying that was what she really needed personally. This need was obvious because as we talked, her son was hitting her leg and tugging at her clothes, using all his energy to demand her attention. She faced great challenges in training her son; a desperate cry for help was written across her face and in her tone of voice.

As our conversation ended and we arrived at our destination, we all stepped out of the subway car. She turned to say she would tell her husband about my leadership book and hoped my parenting book would be available soon. In those few seconds, her son had already run ahead of her, down the crowded stairs, and was out of sight in the midst of a multitude of travelers. The mother frantically turned and chased after him. This incident reinforced my desire to finish this resource to encourage parents and grandparents raising children.

As a father of four children, I take parenting seriously. I believe my greatest responsibility and most lasting impact in this life will result from the parenting of my own children. The strategies in this book are drawn from personal experiences as a child and as a parent raising four children. In addition to personal anecdotes, I have also sought to include some of the best tried-and-true practices from numerous child-training experts, studying the methods of model families that produce mentally, emotionally, and spiritually healthy children and seeking to retain the principles and practices that represent foundational truths. No one person's ideas on child raising are sufficient for all situations. What I strive to achieve in the following thirty-one chapters is to present general principles that can be adapted to fit the unique situations of your own family.

We all need constant encouragement and advice to be successful. My motivation for this book also springs from my own need. I have only a few more years of direct influence in my children's lives. When I began this project, Elizabeth was sixteen, Timothy thirteen, Laura eleven, and Adam seven. With all four children living under one roof, our home was always full of differing emotional, physical, social, and spiritual developmental stages. The next ten years will, in many ways, demonstrate the success or failure of my ability to prepare them for life. No one else has the natural, God-given ability to influence them more than my wife and I. I cannot afford to learn by trial and error. In this important parenting role, every error results in a negative experience or lost opportunity to build up my child. This book serves as my own personal manual for the instruction of my own children. My heart's desire is that this book will also serve you and other parents and grandparents around the world who desire to raise children of distinction.

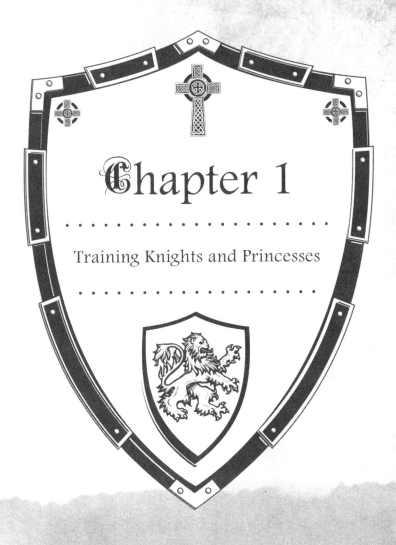

Chapter 1

Training Knights and Princesses

Perhaps in time the so-called Dark Ages will be thought of as including our own.

—Georg Christoph Lichtenberg (1742–1799)

The Medieval Age is similar in some ways to the times we live in today. From that turbulent era in human history, many relevant principles can be gleaned regarding raising our children to become leaders and standards of excellence (knights and princesses). During the Medieval Age, society had reverted to barbaric ways. Most societies' moral standards were base or absent. People were selfishly looking out for their own interests. Most were lovers of pleasure rather than lovers of the common good, hurting one another in order to get ahead. Unfortunately, the passing of time hasn't caused humankind to improve very much, if at all.

Our modern society may be an even darker era than the Medieval Ages, simply because we have many more self-centered people living today, most of whom are packed into large cities around the world. In addition to individual selfishness, the modern media provides a constant stream of immoral, exploitive images. Our children do not need to go looking for trouble—trouble is looking for them. This is indeed a very dark age.

Hope is always present, even in the midst of darkness. In the Middle Ages, children from nobility (knights and princesses) stood out as examples of purity and morality. People who were tired of a filthy, low level of existence could look to these examples as models for a better life. These knights and princesses became the leaders that took their society out of the dark ages.

You can raise your son or daughter to be a knight or princess today. Your children can learn to resist temptation and morally compromising situations. They can learn to have moral values and standards above those of the general populace. In doing so, they also, just as the knights and princesses of old, will serve as examples and leaders for others. They will lead their friends and become a blessing to teachers, students, and parents. Over time, your knight or princess will make a positive difference in this age.

I am sure you desire this for your child, but if you're like most parents, you feel under-prepared for the important role of training your children to become successful adults. When our first child was born, I was so afraid that I would drop her. Keeping her alive, fed, and comfortable (like free from diaper rash) seemed to be all we could handle. Raising her to become a successful adult or a princess seemed a lofty ambition. However, I realized I needed to overcome my insecurities because our little baby was our little baby. She was our responsibility. My wife and I would be the most important influences in her life.

You as a parent are the one who will shape your child's future, more than anyone else in this world. Because you are the most important person in your child's life, you need to become an expert at parenting. You have already studied parenting by watching your parents and grandparents. Experience is a great teacher, but today's challenges are more complex than what you faced when you were a child. You need help and support to raise knights and princesses. You can do this by learning from wisdom as well as from experience. You can train your child to be a knight or princess by beginning to apply the following four points:

1. **Be role models.** Mothers and fathers need to live out what they are teaching. We can't expect our children to develop high values and moral character if they see us modeling the opposite. This doesn't mean that parents have to be perfect, but they do need to be genuine. In the latter part of the Middle Ages, the northern kingdom of Spain issued a decree that a boy could only become a knight if he were the son of a knight. The same is true today. Our children will only become knights or princesses of noble character if we set the example.

2. **Feed them a good diet of heroes.** Tell them about real people who are worth emulating. Read stories of heroes throughout history. When children are young, read positive fictional stories and fairy tales to them that reinforce good values.

3. **Give them your time.** Positive encouragement and quality time are crucial to any good relationship. Your children are unique and need to be encouraged in becoming all they are made to be. Don't push them to become a copy of who you want them to be, but help them become who they are uniquely and powerfully created to be. They have unique skills and talents that can be built upon.

4. **Teach them to be lifelong learners.** A teachable spirit goes a long way in society today. Greatness is not achieved overnight, but is built throughout one's whole life.

The following chapters will paint a picture of what it means to be a knight or princess and will include practical advice on how to raise knights and princesses in this dark age. I would like to finish this opening chapter with a vivid memory from my childhood of my parents' loving, corrective training.

Growing up in a family with four children, I saw my parents' attempts at administering corrective discipline firsthand. My older brother Craig and I were less than two years apart. Craig was by nature more adventurous and mischievous than I. He often complained that he was the first to be blamed. Simply put, he often was blamed first because he was guilty most of the time. His nature was strong and he resisted training. He would describe me as wimpy and quick to do what I was told. He received twice as much discipline as I did, but as a younger brother I followed him in wrongdoing and made some of my own mistakes.

My parents enjoyed retelling the story of when, as young boys, we were caught smoking cigarettes behind a tree. My parents took us home and sat us down at the kitchen table. I was six, and my brother was eight. My father said, "Boys, if you think you are old enough to smoke, I'd better teach you how to do it the right way." He gave each of us a cigarette and told us to begin smoking and to make sure that we inhaled with each puff. After the first puff, I was in tears and asked to leave the table. My brother, on the other hand, smoked his entire cigarette with a smug look on his face. Overconfidence and pride was beaming from his face. At this point, my father and mother wondered if their method of teaching us not to smoke had created an eight-year-old chain-smoker. Fortunately, my father was not one to give up and kept to his plan. He lit another cigarette for my brother. Halfway through the second cigarette, my brother's face lost its smugness and color. As he turned a light shade of green, he ran into the bathroom and threw up. My parents' training had worked.

Often, strong-willed children who are constantly challenging their parents end up becoming leaders. Consistent training in the right course of action will, in time, produce good results. The following chapters should help provide solid advice in training your child to become a knight or princess who blesses others while bringing honor to his or her family.

Application Points:
- What did you learn from this chapter that you would like to implement?
- Which of the four points listed in this chapter would you like to work on, and when would you like to start?
- Who do you need to help you or join with you in order to be successful?

Chapter 2

A Princess Sets the Standard

I am a princess. All girls are. Even if they live in tiny old attics; even if they dress in rags; even if they aren't pretty, or smart, or young. They're still princesses. All of us. Didn't your father ever tell you that? Didn't he?

—Sarah Crewe in *A Little Princess* (1995)

Young girls have wonderful imaginations. They can easily picture themselves as princesses in fairy-tale adventures, traveling to far-away lands, and being rescued by handsome knights or, through their own skill, rescuing others. This world desperately needs young women to act as princesses and to revive and refresh the concept of purity.

People everywhere love purity. They love pure air, pure water, pure food, pure ideals, pure motives, and pure dreams. All of these can be found easily enough, but to find a young girl or woman walking as a pure princess is a rare treasure of great value. If you want to help your daughter protect her purity in this dark age, you will need to be intentional. Their dreams will quickly become their aspirations. This is why it is vital that we help shape our daughters' dreams and aspirations. If we do not help set their course, they will be left to the mercy of the values espoused by TV idols, movie stars, and music icons. The picture parents paint for daughters as ladies of purity and virtue will be a very different one from the message most pop singers and movie stars promote. My wife and I feel a sense of responsibility to raise our daughters to model purity and chastity in this morally dark time in human history. It is our vision to see them go beyond living as pure and lovely ladies of virtue to also leading other young maidens along the path of purity. We believe that our daughters and your daughters can develop a vision of womanhood that is beautiful and exciting.

A princess in the Middle Ages was expected to set the standard for virtue and moral purity. In the same way, modern parents can help daughters develop a vision for their lives as virtuous princesses with high moral standards. The words we choose to use in blessing and instructing our children will have lasting impact. A young girl will believe she is a princess if her parents and loved ones tell her she is. When she believes she is a princess, she will desire to act as a princess. As a girl matures, the world around her will challenge her and work to pull her down. It will take a team of people, such as extended family and mentors, to support and help. Raising a princess in today's environment is no small task, but it is possible. And it is not only possible—it is essential.

> *I think the biggest disease the world suffers from in this day*
> *and age is the disease of people feeling unloved.*
> —Diana, Princess of Wales

As I mentioned, most girls enjoy imagining themselves as a princess. They picture themselves in flowing gowns, receiving attention from a daring and handsome prince. Their natural female design enjoys being cherished and protected. This is first modeled by their mothers and further established in their relationship with their father. Dads, you are the ones who come to the rescue and protect them when they are afraid. What a great privilege it is to be the protector of our daughters.

In addition to fathers, brothers can also play a crucial role in the formation of a young girl's self-esteem. Girls' relationships with their father and brothers can help develop their view of men as protectors and providers. My girls still light up when I tell them they look pretty. I make it a point to compliment their character and the choices they make, but I also compliment them on their appearance. Fathers and mothers help develop a girl's sense of security and self-confidence.

As your daughter enters the teen years, it will be very important that she knows what she believes and why she believes it. Below are three principles for young girls to learn; these are three principles for virtuous living. Women, along with men, are created to rule and subdue this earth by attaining the unique design they were created to fulfill (Genesis 1:27–28). To do this, women must learn to love purity, live valiantly, and serve sacrificially.

As the foundation of these principles, young women must learn that greatness begins in the heart and comes from vision. Daily actions make a difference in the person they become. God can be trusted to reward right choices, even when no one is watching.

Love Purity

Good ideals are not enough unless they are followed through with action. In order to live a pure life, a girl will have to abstain from many activities. At times, such sacrifices will be difficult. The desire to fit in and be popular will challenge her convictions. I have met many girls who started out with high ideals but grew tired of feeling different. They slowly gave in to compromise and chose to fit in. The easy road they thought they were taking soon produced unexpected difficulties and even more compromises. They were no longer suffering for their high ideals and commitment to live purely. Now they were suffering for their choice to fit in and be average. Life is difficult regardless of the road our children choose. One road leads to greatness and blessing for self and others. The other road offers short-term comfort and acceptance, but delivers few lasting blessings to self or others.

Live Valiantly

To live valiantly, your daughter must have confidence and self-respect. These traits are best developed from a strong relationship with Mom and Dad. Words of affirmation regarding who you believe your daughter to be are the building blocks of self-respect. In our home, our kids know they are to be a blessing. I regularly thank them when they are a blessing to us as parents and to their siblings or friends. I also remind them when they are going to spend time with friends that focusing only on themselves will cause them to be insecure. If they look for someone to help or be kind to, they will be happier and will bless another person.

This trait is best learned by watching more than listening. Your children need to see you making valiant choices and doing things that bless others. For example, when you struggle with a hard choice but choose to do what is right regardless of the potential consequence, you are living valiantly. When situations like this happen, tell your children about them. Help them see what it means to live valiantly in a world that wants everyone to fit in.

I also enjoy teaching this principle through superhero movies. They serve as great examples of valiant living. Just the other night our daughter said it used to bother her when I "always" critiqued movies with them as to the good and bad values portrayed. I also highlighted the hidden messages that most movies contained. In time, I stopped telling them and asked them to tell me the good, bad, and hidden messages. My daughter mentioned that she is glad I took the time to train her because now she knows what she believes. Our kids may never save the world like superheroes, but they may be seen as a hero to the friends they help.

Serve Sacrificially

Children can learn how to serve and to offer hospitality. I am amazed at how generous kids can be at times. They don't naturally know the cost or value of things. But they do desire to please those they love. So they will be generous with their time and possessions if we train them how to give generously. At first they will use your money to buy gifts for friends or give away toys that you previously purchased. At such times we need to resist the urge to stop them (within reason), but rather encourage their generosity. In addition to giving generously of possessions, they also need to give generously of their time. They will learn to serve others by serving them with you. When you are helping others or offering hospitality in your home, make sure you let your children help. In so doing, they will learn to be hospitable.

In addition to parents, role models can play a significant role in helping daughters to love purity, live valiantly, and serve sacrificially. Many parents today are distraught as they watch their children choose role models from actresses and musicians with low moral values. Actively connecting our daughters with potential role models is one way parents can influence their children. This will seem very natural if introduced early in a girl's life. She will look forward to the extra attention, and it will be very important when she reaches her early teen years. The teen years are usually when children begin questioning parental values. Mentors can serve as additional voices into our child's life during this formative time. With the help of a community, it is possible to train our daughters in purity, valiant living, and sacrificial service. They can find joy in honoring their parents by their speech, chaste behavior, and dress. The following is a story of a lost princess and how she learned what it really meant to be a princess.

The Lost Princess

Once upon a time in a small country named Puran, there lived a king, queen, and their precious daughter. During their reign as king and queen, the Russian empire to the east was in great turmoil. The peasants had revolted, and the unrest quickly spread to neighboring countries. The Kingdom of Puran was no exception. In just one week, the rebel forces seized control of the capital city and surrounded the royal palace. The king and queen, with their two-year-old daughter Anna, prepared to evacuate. Before they made their escape, the rebel forces broke through their defenses and stormed the palace. In an attempt to save others' lives, the king and queen went out to meet the invading rebels. They left their little princess in the care of her nurse, Mina.

The arrival of the king and queen did little to slow the attack. Instead, the rebels seized them and bound them with ropes. On seeing that the king and queen were captured, the nurse hid the princess in a large bundle of clothing. Then she fled the palace with her bundle amidst the chaos of looters and fleeing palace servants.

Mina knew the little princess would only be safe if her identity was kept hidden. She dressed the princess in peasant clothing and cut her hair short and shaggy. With the little princess looking more like a poor peasant boy than a member of the royal family, they left the capital in search of a quiet country village in which to hide. The new rebel government took power and, rather than kill the king and queen, exiled them for ransom, paid by wealthy noble relatives in Western Europe. The king and queen hoped their little princess was safe, but they had no way of knowing. Since there was no way to search for the princess without putting her at further risk, they prayed and waited for a time to return to their country and find their lost daughter.

In order to protect the little princess, Mina taught Anna to call her Auntie Mina. Mina loved the little princess and determined to raise her to be the princess she really was. Mina mended clothes and baked to provide for their daily needs. As the little princess grew, she learned to sew and to bake wonderful cakes and breads herself. She also learned how to clean the house and keep things in order. Singing and storytelling were her specialties, and she was a constant joy to Mina.

The cottage they occupied appeared shabby on the outside, but inside it was rich and full of singing, love, and laughter. They had very little in terms of material possessions, but there were many in the village much poorer than themselves. The new government had not created a better life for anyone in the kingdom, and many villagers secretly began talking about bringing back the king. Until Anna's parents returned, though, Mina was not going to reveal the princess' identity. While they waited, Mina and Anna did what they could to help those poorer than themselves. Anna would regularly take bread and cakes to poor children and widows. In this, she learned to set a good example by serving compassionately and selflessly.

To be continued at the end of each chapter...

Application points:
- What did you learn from this chapter that you would like to implement?
- How can you teach your daughter to love purity, live valiantly, and serve sacrificially?
- Who could you introduce as a mentor for your daughter?

Chapter 3

Princess Warriors

Very fair was [Eowyn's] face, and her long hair was like a river of gold. Slender and tall she was in her white robe girt with silver; but strong she seemed and stern as steel, a daughter of kings.

—J. R. R. Tolkien, *The Two Towers*

Our daughters need to learn that there will be times when they need to fight for themselves and for others. They may enjoy imagining themselves as a damsel in distress waiting for a handsome knight, but there will be times when they must stand up for what is right and be the one who fights injustice. Our daughters will learn how to fight for what is right mostly by watching their parents.

"A Maidens Call"
by R.F.

Young maidens rest in peaceful states,
growing in stature and gentle grace.
Though soft and pure appearance be,
strength of character is forged in thee.

The strength you'll find that's strong and true:
the Lamb of God who lives in you.
Fear not when times of testing come,
the source of power is Christ, the Son.

Battles are fought not with fists and bows,
nor with tongues that cut with evil blows,
but with purity, truth, and ample grace,
bringing hope and joy to the sullen face.

Rise up and go forth in His name,
fear not any earthly stain.
For evil lurks and battles sure,
will tarnish not thy maidens pure.

The call goes out: maidens far and wide,
"Stand strong this day and do not hide."
The time for pure, strong maidens has come,
a time to celebrate—THY will being done.

In addition to standing up for others, we need to teach our daughters when it is appropriate for them to protect themselves. This can be especially hard for nice girls who have wonderful servant hearts. Kindness, hospitality, servanthood, and humility are wonderful traits that should be practiced in the appropriate environments. Nice girls who learn to please others may have a hard time saying no. In the wrong situation, they can be taken advantage of or even harmed. It is sad to hear stories of wonderful girls marrying abusive husbands. Nice girls fall for the trap of trying to save bad boys and end up getting hurt.

As parents we need to teach our daughters how to say no. We need to teach them to stand on principles even when it upsets or offends someone. Teach her that being nice is important, but not more important than safety. It is also important to teach our children how to say no to morally compromising situations. Our oldest daughter recently returned to China from the United States after her freshman year at college. She was nineteen years old and traveling alone. Let me just say that I am glad she knows how to say no. I will let Elizabeth tell the story in her own words:

> This wasn't my first time traveling alone. I had traveled on international flights by myself before. But when a random young man approached me on the plane, I was completely caught off guard. I had noticed this same guy staring at me in the airport before boarding, but had quickly dismissed the incident, choosing not to make it a big deal in my mind.
>
> Once boarding the plane, I found my seat, row 24 on the aisle. I was sitting comfortably in my seat, reading. The first hour of my ten-hour flight had passed uneventfully when I noticed out of the corner of my eye someone squat down in the aisle. I turned in my seat and saw that it was the same young man from the airport—and he was talking to me.

He started off with a typical American greeting: "Hi. How are ya?"

At that moment, I don't think I even knew the answer to that question. The main question in my mind was, *Where is this going?*

I looked at him, wide-eyed and wary, and slowly responded, "Fine..."

He continued his introduction. He seemed a little shaky to me—probably because he had just come up and started talking to some girl on the airplane. He didn't appear creepy. He was in his mid-twenties, in good shape, and not at all bad looking. But his physical appearance didn't negate the fact that he was a complete stranger and I was traveling alone. Squatting in an airplane aisle so you can talk to someone isn't exactly a natural approach to friendship.

"So, this is a really long flight, and I was wondering if you wanted to sit next to me and chat for a little bit."

"Uhhhh..."

The shock must have shown on my face because he quickly acknowledged that I seemed uncomfortable. "You're not the type to talk to strangers, are you?" he (teasingly) asked.

I laughed. "No, I'm not." *Especially random young men*, I said in my head. I didn't want to be rude, but I knew I couldn't lead him to think I appreciated the attention he was showing me. Everything my parents had ever warned me about strange men flooded my mind as this man continued to make small talk. I was taught that being a godly and nice girl means being tough sometimes, taking precautions to avoid compromising or unsafe situations. And in some situations, showing the proper precaution may appear rude or mean.

After a few minutes, I think he caught the hint. "So you're not interested in talking, are you?"

"No, I'm not. It's nothing personal...but I don't know you."

He seemed to take that relatively well, especially for such an obvious rejection. It must take guts to squat down next to a random girl and ask her to come and talk to you.

He stood up. "Well, enjoy your trip!"

"You too! Enjoy China," I added.

He chuckled and shook his head. "Oh, I hate China."

That caught me off guard. I just told him how I had grown up in China, and now he tells me he hates China? Even if I had been interested in talking to him, that would have turned me off right away. I had to laugh to myself once he left. What a strange occurrence.

Now, I would be lying if I said that special attention from a relatively attractive young man didn't make me feel flattered. It's a bit of an ego boost to have a stranger pick you out as someone to flirt with. But that little emotion isn't important enough to risk my safety.

Many girls would be afraid to turn down a young man's approach. If a girl struggles at all with whether she is attractive or not (and pretty much all girls do), she will most likely be afraid to turn down someone who finds her good-looking. And if a girl is really sweet, she may be afraid to reject the guy because he may be "deeply and incurably hurt" by her rejection. Even though both of these struggles are legitimate and common for young women, girls need to learn that they are not worth risking their safety. Ultimately, there are times when nice girls have to appear mean.

It is possible that talking to this young man would have been an innocent diversion. However, opening the door for a relationship with a strange young man on a plane would put Elizabeth in a place of vulnerability. Having said this, my daughter does step into some hard situations with the proper support. Today she is visiting prostitutes with a ministry that helps girls trapped in the sex industry to get off the streets and start new lives. It is not the safest environment, but she is not entering it without the proper support around her for safety and success. Too many true stories of rape, abduction, and abuse exist in our modern society. We need to teach our daughters how to keep themselves out of compromising situations in the first place. Nice girls who don't know how to say no fall for bad boyfriends, get pregnant, and sometimes die too early.

Princess warriors show discretion in the fights they choose to fight. They are willing to say no to their friends, do not put themselves in compromising or unsafe situations, and submit themselves to parents and other appropriate authority figures. Teaching our daughters to say no is an important part of preparing them for success in this dark age.

The Princess Warrior

Time passed slowly in the poor village, and Anna celebrated her seventh birthday. Though more and more people all over the kingdom were talking about ousting the rebel government and bringing back the king, it still had not come to pass. One day when Anna was returning home from school, she saw a group of children along the path that were a little older than her. They were picking on a new girl that had just moved to the village. The new girl was very poorly dressed, and the children were making fun of her. Anna was outraged that these older children would be so cruel to the new girl. In spite of the fact that she was younger and smaller than the other children, Anna stepped between them and told them how badly they were behaving.

"How dare you say mean things to this little princess," she said. "Her clothes may not look like those of a princess, but I can see on the inside that she really is royalty."

The older children were taken aback by how strongly Anna had rebuked them. They decided that teasing the new girl wasn't fun anymore and left to find some other mischief elsewhere. However, as they went, they said terrible things about Anna and pelted her with dirt and small stones, making Anna's old dress look even older and muddier.

The new girl thanked Anna for saving her and for declaring that she was a princess on the inside. Anna walked her new friend home and talked more about how little princesses need to speak kind words and do kind deeds for others. In no time at all, Anna had formed a steadfast group of virtuous girlfriends that were learning how to act like princesses.

Application points:

- What did you learn from this chapter that you would like to implement?
- In what situations do you need to prepare your daughters to say no?
- What age-appropriate stories or examples can you share with your daughter in order to help her be a princess warrior?

Chapter 4

A Princess Sets the Example
in Action and Speech

"Beauty is truth, truth beauty"—that is all
Ye know on earth, and all ye need to know.

—John Keats, *Ode on a Grecian Urn*

As our daughters grow in character, they can set excellent examples for the next generation of young girls. I was so thankful for the influence that a young teenager had on our girls when they were preteens. Michelle was fourteen years old when she started babysitting once a week. She would show up at our door with a bag filled with little books or special toys for our kids to play with while my wife and I enjoyed going out on a date. (A weekly date night with your spouse is something I highly recommend; it was a chance for us to connect in an uninterrupted way that made the rest of the week run so much more smoothly.) For our children, it was a time to enjoy the special attention and energy that Michelle brought into the home. Michelle was a wonderful example of modesty and kindness. When my oldest daughter turned eleven, Michelle started a weekly gathering for young girls to talk, read the Bible, and have fun. This was a great confidence builder and reinforcement of the values we wanted our daughter to embrace. I was excited to see that when my own daughter became an older teen, she started a similar group for the preteen girls. Michelle's servant heart made it easy for my daughter to follow her example and reach out to younger girls.

In order for our daughters to lead by example, they need to develop character worth following. Michelle's parents helped her build her character in a way that became a blessing to many other families. Character is something that takes time to develop. Right materials and good examples of virtuous living are food for character building, but our children build their own character one good decision at a time.

> *Parents can only give good advice or put their children on the*
> *right paths, but the final forming of a person's character lies*
> *in their own hands.*
> —Anne Frank

The right building blocks for character involve teaching proper standards, setting high ideals, practicing consistent discipline, offering loving correction, and giving moral guidance. When we provide these building blocks for character, our children have the opportunity to become examples to others in thought, word, and deed.

A princess' lips are sweet

One way a girl's character is displayed is by the way she communicates. Words are especially important for girls. Women in general interact with their world through words. As a result, training them to be pure in the way they talk and speak of others is very important. I like the following advice:

> *Whoever would love life*
> *and see good days*
> *must keep his tongue from evil*
> *and his lips from deceitful speech.*
> *He must turn from evil and do good;*
> *he must seek peace and pursue it.*
> *For the eyes of the Lord are on the righteous*
> *and his ears are attentive to their prayer,*
> *but the face of the Lord is against those who do evil.*
> —1 Peter 3:10–12

One of the first encouragements in this verse is to keep your tongue from evil. It is easy to underestimate the power of our words. As a child, I learned the phrase: "Sticks and stones will break my bones, but words will never hurt me." In my opinion, the phrase should go like this: "Sticks and stones will break your bones, but words hurt more than anything." Some people spend their whole life trying to overcome hurtful words spoken to them. Without forgiveness, such hurtful memories grow into bitterness. Have you seen the devastating impact that bitterness has on a person physically and emotionally? Bitterness can manifest itself in actual physical illness. Hurtful words can destroy marriages, separate close friends, divide families, and undermine stability in companies or churches.

If we, from an early age, train our daughter to keep her tongue from evil and to speak kind, edifying words to others, she can make a difference in her lifetime. Show me a girl who listens sympathetically, speaks life-giving compliments, and encourages with words, and I will show you a girl who will change her world. She will also enjoy many close friendships, for people love being around those who truly listen, encourage, and build up.

Girls should also be taught how to speak appropriately to people of different ages. Careless speech can show lack of respect to adults and will affect her personal reputation. A girl who learns to control her speech and uses gentle, clear, appropriate tones will gain the respect and admiration of others.

As I wrote this last statement, my youngest daughter was reading over my shoulder and asked, "What about a girl with a strong personality? Does she also need to learn to talk in gentle, clear, and appropriate tones?" I thought about her question and became convinced that the principle still applies. It is especially important for girls who are naturally strong and outgoing to learn how to control their speech.

Telling a woman that she is a great speaker or a wonderful communicator is a compliment and would be well received. But most would not feel complimented if told they have a loud voice. Positive feedback is usually given to those who have outgoing personalities and have mastered the art of speech. They are not the product of untrained or uncontrolled speech. Uncontrolled and flippant words so often are hurtful to others and damaging to the one who uses them. Words may not cut into the flesh like a knife, but, like razor-sharp swords, they cut deep into the heart. The old rule "think twice before you speak once" would save most of us a lot of heartache.

> *Do not let any unwholesome talk come out of your mouths,*
> *but only what is helpful for building others up according to*
> *their needs, that it may benefit those who listen. And do not*
> *grieve the Holy Spirit of God, with whom you were sealed*

for the day of redemption. Get rid of all bitterness, rage and anger, brawling and slander, along with every form of malice. Be kind and compassionate to one another, forgiving each other, just as in Christ God forgave you.
—Ephesians 4:29–32

Gossip is another type of communication that should not be part of a princess' speech. It is natural to be interested in what others are doing, and talking about such things is not wrong. However, when the conversation is mixed with a desire to hurt or devalue another, it becomes gossip. I enjoy teaching college students how to spread what I call "good gossip." In this exercise, I ask them during the next day or two to tell someone else about something they like or admire about one of their fellow classmates. Then, in class, I ask them to share the good gossip they have heard. It is a wonderful way to get others spreading good, encouraging, life-giving words about others. When a girl finds herself in a group that is gossiping about another person, she should leave after saying something positive about the person being talked about. Her comment could change the nature of the conversation.

The inward beauty of a gentle and quiet spirit is admired and sought after. The picture of a mother comforting her child is common around the world. Women are naturally seen as loving, caring, and self-sacrificing. This is what our daughters can become with the right encouragement. Have you ever met a beautiful woman who shocked you by her foul language or mean spirit? It is amazing how quickly her outward beauty is no longer visible. The proverb in Luke 6:45 states truth: "For out of the overflow of his heart his mouth speaks." Scary indeed is a woman who possesses outward beauty but inwardly lacks character and kindness. Just consider the female villains in movies and children's fables who are beautiful women but have chosen cruelty over kindness. They can be wearing the most beautiful dresses with glittering jewels, but their lack of inward character and cold heart turns them into scary villains.

A princess is pure
In addition to helping our daughters develop character, we also need to prepare them to protect their moral purity. Compromise in the area of

sexual purity creates emotional damage, low self-esteem, and hurt. She may gain the attention of the young man she desires, but not for her inner qualities. Her moral compromise reduces her to a sex object. One proverb wisely states, "Like a gold ring in a pig's snout is a beautiful woman who shows no discretion" (Proverbs 11:22).

Young women can be encouraged to show discretion in their actions and appearance. Our daughter's inward beauty will naturally enhance her natural feminine beauty. Let us encourage our princesses to grow in character through their pure lives, kind speech, and strong moral character.

The Lesson of Purity

As Anna grew older, she enjoyed playing with the village children and attending the local school. She blended in well with the other children—even a little too well at times. One day, she came home and told Mina that she wanted to wear some clothes that were not modest, even for a girl as young as Anna. She also began using inappropriate words and forgot her manners when addressing adults.

Mina sat down with Anna and shared with her the virtue of modesty, a cherished virtue of all princesses. Mina said, "All little princesses, like you and your friends, should learn to dress modestly in a way that shows respect for yourselves and emphasizes your purity. You must also watch what you say. The words you speak are a reflection of your heart. Little princesses should have hearts full of good thoughts so that their words will come out polite, generous, kind, pure, and respectful. Words are very important for building others up, but they can also be very powerful in hurting people."

Anna began to understand that her beauty needed to come from within her and not from the clothes she wore or anything else on the outside. Anna internalized the virtues of modesty and purity well and in the following weeks convinced many of her friends to talk and dress more like princesses and to respect purity.

Application points:

- What did you learn from this chapter that you would like to implement?
- Has your daughter established any patterns of talking or dressing that should be corrected?
- Who can support you in training your daughter to model purity and speak graciously?

Chapter 5

A Princess Enjoys Beauty

A thing of beauty is a joy forever:
its loveliness increases;
it will never pass into nothingness.

—John Keats, *Endymion*

She walks in beauty, like the night
Of cloudless climes and starry skies;
And all that's best of dark and bright
Meet in her aspect and her eyes...
Where thoughts serenely sweet express
How pure, how dear their dwelling-place.

And on that cheek, and o'er that brow,
So soft, so calm, yet eloquent,
The smiles that win, the tints that glow,
But tell of days in goodness spent,
A mind at peace with all below,
A heart whose love is innocent!
—Lord George Gordon Byron,
She Walks in Beauty

Lord Byron describes a beauty that goes beyond physical beauty and speaks of a peaceful mind and innocent heart. Girls are natural lovers of beauty. From the time they are small, they are drawn to beautiful flowers, homes, dresses, or faces. They also enjoy the compliments of adults who tell them how beautiful they look ...like a little princess.

I remember a time when my second daughter performed in a play. All dressed up like an angel with her curly blond hair and cute smile, she did look like a real little angel. As she was waiting to perform, I overheard one of the adult helpers say to her, "Honey, you don't have to do anything, just stand there and look pretty." This was a well-meaning compliment, but not the advice I have for my daughters. I don't want my daughters to be background props or cut flowers on display—beautiful, but lacking substance. I remind my own daughters that being truly beautiful involves so much more than physical appearance. We can do little to change the physical appearance we have received, but there is a lot we can do to become beautiful people. Physical beauty is a small part of what makes a woman truly beautiful.

> *Your beauty should not come from outward adornment,*
> *such as braided hair and the wearing of gold jewelry and*
> *fine clothes. Instead, it should be that of your inner self, the*
> *unfading beauty of a gentle and quiet spirit, which is of great*
> *worth in God's sight.*
> —1 Peter 3:3–4

I don't see anything wrong with wearing nice clothes and appropriate jewelry or getting hair styled, but this is not the source of a girl's beauty. Pretty clothes are something that girls naturally enjoy. This a wonderful part of growing up as a woman, but the inner beauty of moral character, kind speech, gentleness, and a quiet spirit will far outshine physical beauty. True beauty is not having a beautiful face, but a beautiful heart. A girl with a lovely personality and pure heart may not attract constant attention from young men, but in the course of time, her beauty will be seen and appreciated.

> *...true beauty is not of the face, but of the soul. There is*
> *a beauty so deep and lasting that it will shine out of the*
> *homeliest face and make it pretty. This is the beauty to be*
> *first sought and admired. It is a quality of the mind and*
> *heart and is manifested in word and deed. A happy heart,*
> *a smiling face, loving words and deeds, and a desire to be of*
> *service, will make any girl beautiful.*
> —Mabel Hale, *Beautiful Girlhood* [1]

Girls naturally want to be pretty. Girls should learn to seek goodness and purity first so that they have a kind and generous heart. Then it is appropriate for them to make their outward appearance match the beauty of their heart. The problem is when a girl sets her sights on looking like the girls in magazines or movies. A girl who can accept herself and appreciate herself for the good qualities she possesses has greater self-confidence than most supermodels, who only own fading physical beauty. "But godliness with contentment is great gain" (1 Timothy 6:6) applies to how we look as well as how many possessions we have.

Another wonderful aspect of womanhood is to enjoy the richness of colorful clothing and sweet fragrances. Women are often good at the delicate art of pampering. Little girls naturally love to be pampered with nice-smelling lotions, bath oils, and pretty-colored clothes. The art of taking care of oneself, however, requires training. My wife is good at reminding young mothers to take time to care for themselves physically and spiritually. It is very difficult for many young mothers to find time for themselves when young children demand constant attention. When moms learn to care for themselves, their children and husbands benefit by having a healthier, happier wife and mother. When mothers set this example, daughters can be trained in serving others and at the same time can learn how to care for themselves.

Young girls must be trained in good grooming habits. A young woman who is clean and neat with a joyful continence is in a good place to be a blessing to others. Children can learn to enjoy good grooming habits when they are young. I enjoy seeing the smile on kids' faces when they emerge from a bath with clean hair and shiny skin. When our children were little, I would ask to smell their hair and loved the fresh smell of my clean children. They would wait for me to tell them they smelled good. We recently had friends from western China staying with us on their way back to America. They are blessed with four girls and one baby boy. I asked their youngest daughter, four years old and fresh from the bath, if I could smell her wet hair, and she immediately walked over and bowed her head so I could get a good sniff. She enjoyed showing off her clean hair, and I enjoyed seeing her smiling confidence as I commented on how good her fresh, clean hair smelled. Moments like this train little girls to appreciate personal cleanliness. A girl well trained will consider cleanliness, neatness, and cheerful countenance as part of who they are. Trained in this way, she will be appreciated by her neighbors, siblings, and friends. Cleanliness and neatness open the door to offer hospitality. It is hard for others to enjoy your hospitality if your person and home are in disorder.

Hospitality is another wonderful way for ladies to share their kindness with others. It is a time when privacy is put aside and we are able to serve others. Hospitality is much more of an attitude of service than having a fancy home or extravagant food to place before guests. A little princess must be trained on how to excel in serving through hospitality. The following story provides an insightful illustration:

> In the cloakroom of a certain school, a question arose among some girls as to who had the most beautiful hands. The teacher listened to the girls thoughtfully. They compared hands and shared secrets of keeping them pretty. Amanda said that a girl could not keep perfect hands and wash dishes, or sweep. Marcia spoke of the evil effects of cold and wind and too much sunshine. Francis told of her favorite lotion. Phillipa spoke of proper manicuring. At last the teacher spoke.
>
> "To my mind, Jennifer Higgins has the most beautiful hands of any girl in school," she said quietly.
>
> "Jennie Higgins!" exclaimed Amanda in amazement. "Why, her hands are rough and red and look as if she took no care of them. I never thought of them as beautiful."
>
> "I have seen those hands carrying dainty food to the sick and soothing the brow of the aged. She is her widowed mother's main help. She does the milking and carries the wood and water, yes, and washes dishes night and morning, that her mother may save the hard work. I have never known her to be too tired to speak kindly to her little sister and help her in her play. I have found those busy hands helping her brother with his kite. I tell you, I think they are the most beautiful hands I have ever seen, for they are always busy helping somewhere."[2]

This is the type of beauty I try to encourage my daughters to develop. We have all been given natural talents and gifts to share. Let us encourage our daughters to use their gifts to serve others and in so doing make themselves truly beautiful.

Flowers and Lace

As time passed, Mina grew confident that Anna's identity was safely hidden. She realized that though they could not live richly like in the palace, they could still make their home beautiful. Songs, stories, and laughter were important for having a happy home, but beauty and orderliness were also vital to that happiness. So Mina began teaching Anna how to arrange the table at suppertime to be beautiful. Anna loved making elegant flower arrangements for the table from wildflowers in the fields. Mina and Anna together sewed beautiful tablecloths and wall hangings. Soon their little cottage, though simple on the outside, was fast becoming a palace on the inside.

To Anna's delight, Mina made her a dress from fabric as blue as the sky and finished it with white silk lace. When Anna first wore the dress, she expected to see a big smile on Mina's face. Although Mina was very proud of Anna, on Mina's face was the look of fear. For standing before her, with curly brown hair falling down over her shoulders in a beautiful dress, Anna looked too much like the real princess that she truly was. Mina feared others would see the real princess she was so desperately trying to hide. Up to this time, Mina had only told Anna that her parents were taken away during the rebellion, but she hadn't told her they were the king and queen. She was afraid this secret would be too difficult for a little girl to keep. At the right time, Mina determined to tell Anna that she was the real princess. But doing so now would only bring trouble and danger upon them.

Mina convinced Anna to only wear the dress inside the cottage. Anna was so happy with her new dress that it was easy for her to obey. In spite of Mina's fears, it made her heart rejoice to see little Anna dressed as beautifully as a princess.

Application points:

- What did you learn from this chapter about beauty that you would like to implement?
- In what ways can you begin to train your daughter in beauty?
- When would you like to start?

Chapter 6

A Princess Models
Selflessness and Humility

*Do you wish to be great? Then begin by being little. Do
you desire to construct a vast and lofty fabric? Think first
about the foundations of humility; the higher your
structure is to be, the deeper must be its foundation.*

—Saint Augustine

Modern society encourages women to be proud, daring, and full of self-esteem, promoting equality and fighting for her rights. Women are urged not to let anyone tell them what they can and can't do simply because they are women. There are certainly many examples when women have been suppressed throughout history. It is important for women to seek opportunities to reach their full potential in environments that encourage their gifts and abilities. However, the militant attitude that teaches young women to see the world as oppressive will not create a lady of virtue. My wife and I have been cheated and robbed, put down, slighted, and slandered. These situations have caused us pain, but they have not caused us to become distrusting of everyone. We have had to remind ourselves that we would rather be stolen from than steal. We would rather be lied to and deceived on occasion than become untrusting. It is important to teach our daughters how to keep a positive perspective and a serving heart.

> *Do not think of yourself more highly than you ought, but*
> *rather think of yourself with sober judgment, in accordance*
> *with the measure of faith God has given you.*
> —Romans 12:3

Proper perspective is especially challenging for daughters entering their teen years. So much is happening in her body, life, and emotions. It is hard for her to keep up with her changing body and feelings, let alone think about others. This is an easy time for selfishness to arise as a result of insecurity and fear. She may want to focus more on her issues and forget that others have problems and concerns of their own. Selfishness will make her feel like she needs the latest styles, even though it costs more than the family normally spends. As loving parents, we can help our daughters overcome selfishness at different developmental stages of their lives. Teaching our daughter how to fight selfishness is part of helping her grow into a beautiful woman. Humility is one of the character qualities one can use to fight selfishness.

Training our daughter in humility will actually increase her feeling of significance. Humility is seeing ourselves for who we really are. We do want to praise our children for their accomplishments, but we don't want them to feel superior to others. Our children know they naturally excel at some things and not at others. They can be encouraged to improve, compete, and strive to grow, but not in a proud way. If our praise of children only involves grades, winning first place, or beating their classmates, they can become arrogant and insecure at the same time. It is easy for them to secretly fear they are loved based on how well they perform. The world rewards in this way, but children seek and deserve unconditional love from their parents.

If our children develop a feeling of superiority or pride, they become self-centered. Pride drives friendships away and can cause our children to feel isolated. We can train our children to see themselves as special and talented and still teach humility. They need to appreciate that their friends also have qualities worthy of praise. A self-centered child, even with a great deal of self-confidence, can be a very lonely child. A talented but humble child who knows how to serve and care for others will excel in life and friendships. Humility brings with it a sense of peace and security. A humble person is not self-absorbed and fears less what others are thinking about them because they are thinking of helping others. This type of humility will come with great rewards.

You can make more friends in two months by becoming
genuinely interested in other people than you can in two years
by trying to get others interested in you.
—Dale Carnegie,
How to Win Friends and Influence People

The famous author Oswald Chambers said in *My Utmost for His Highest,* "It is not a question of our equipment but of our poverty, not of what we bring with us but what God puts into us." God has given our daughters a great number of gifts. Gifts that are given to us should instill in us gratitude and not pride. They should not be used to make us feel more important than others, but rather used to bless others.

As I mentioned earlier, I enjoy watching superhero movies with my children from time to time. Just the other day we went to see *Thor*, a story of the legendary Norse god of thunder. What I enjoyed most about the movie was the interaction between Thor and the people on earth who found him. As the son of a king of another land, he spoke with confidence in a regal manner. His speech seemed a little out of place, but by treating people with respect he seemed to elevate the quality of normal life. He started out as proud and self-centered, but slowly learned to serve others with his strength. In the same way, when we realize our worth as God's children, we can serve others out of the strength of who we are.

> *For we are God's handiwork, created in Christ Jesus to do*
> *good works, which God prepared in advance for us to do.*
> —Ephesians 2:10

The Princess in the Palace

After seven long years of poor leadership and oppression, the people grew so upset with the rebel government that they revolted. They secretly sent for the king and queen and restored them to their thrones. After reclaiming the throne, the king's first matter of importance was to send out an edict searching for his long-lost daughter. Anyone who knew of the princess' whereabouts was to immediately bring her back to the palace. The royal family promised a great reward for the safe return of their daughter.

On the following day, more than fifty young girls dressed as young princesses awaited interviews. They all wanted to be chosen as the lost princess. They all had beautiful curly brown hair and were about the same age as the lost princess. However, no one knew, other than the king, queen, and Mina, about the diamond-shaped birthmark at the back of her head, just below the hairline, that could identify the real princess.

When Mina heard that the king and queen had returned, she packed up Anna's blue dress and set off for the palace. Anna was excited by the adventure of their trip and was even more excited to get a chance to see a real palace. When Mina arrived at the castle, she became very anxious. She feared the king and queen might not be happy with how she had raised Anna, so she decided to let Anna wait in line with the other girls to meet her parents on her own.

"I will return in three days," said Mina.

"But where am I to stay?" asked Anna.

"Once you meet the king and queen, everything will be all right. They will have a place for you."

So Anna stood in line wearing her beautiful blue dress, like all the other little princesses waiting to see the king and queen. The line was long, and while she waited, a young delivery boy came by on his way to the kitchen. He was struggling to balance a large bushel of vegetables in his arms. As he passed Anna, he lost his balance and all the vegetables spilled across the ground. The other little girls in line just laughed at him, but Anna took pity on the servant boy and helped him pick up the vegetables and even carried them to the kitchen with him.

Once in the kitchen, she saw people rushing about to prepare the meals for the king and his guests. The smell of bread and cakes filled the room. Anna was tired of waiting in line and decided to help the bakers prepare their delicacies. She sang while she worked, and everyone in the kitchen was calmed by her sweet-sounding voice. She brought smiles to all their faces, relieving the stress and worry about the day ahead.

Anna was having such a good time in the kitchen that she forgot to pay attention to the hour, and her chance for visiting the king and queen had passed. The chief baker felt sad that this little princess didn't get to see the king and queen, so he arranged for her to serve desserts to the king following the evening meal. Dressed in her beautiful blue dress with the silky lace, she carried sweet cakes, which she herself had made that day, to the king. The queen, exhausted from the interviews, had already gone to bed.

When Anna saw the king, she immediately fell in love with his kind but sad eyes. After serving the cakes, she asked the king.

"Would you like me to sing a song for you before I return to the kitchen?"

"I would like that very much!" answered the king.

The king, even after a long day with little princesses, was very impressed by the daughter of the kitchen staff (for he had assumed that's who she was). Her song soothed his soul, and after the song she told him a story that made him laugh. He hadn't laughed like that in many years. Anna saw that the king was tired, and so, excusing herself, she returned to the kitchen. Anna's heart filled with a new unexplainable excitement that even made her forget the growing longing she felt for her own parents. Once back in the kitchen, she suddenly realized she had nowhere to go. The kitchen staff gladly had her spend the night and helped her reserve a good place in line the next morning.

The next day, Anna quickly realized the girls standing near the front of the line were very snobby and pushy. One girl became so agitated that she tore the dress of another innocent little girl who accidentally had stepped on her foot. The sad little girl, with tears filling her eyes, slowly walked away, for she knew she could no longer see the king and queen in a torn dress. Anna's heart felt so bad for the little girl that she insisted they trade dresses so she could wear her brand-new blue dress with white lace. Then Anna again returned to the kitchen to help those serving the king.

The kitchen staff was glad to have her back and began calling her the little princess (for that is what she was to them). She had won their hearts with her kind and beautiful spirit. Anna decided to give up on waiting in line for the interview since she was able to serve the king desserts in the evenings instead. She thought Mina wouldn't mind as long as Anna told her that she was able to see them. And so she waited for Mina and served the king and queen while blessing all those in the kitchen with her joyful spirit.

Application points:

- What did you learn from this chapter about selflessness and humility that you would like to implement?
- What special gifts or qualities does your child possess?
- How can you encourage your daughter to use these gifts and qualities to bless others?

Chapter 7

A Princess Needs Her Dad

Love is not love
Which alters when it alteration finds,
Or bends with the remover to remove:
O, no! it is an ever-fixed mark...
Love alters not with his brief hours and weeks,
But bears it out even to the edge of doom.
If this be error and upon me proved,
I never writ, nor no man ever loved.

—William Shakespeare, *Sonnet CXVI*

The type of love Shakespeare speaks of is seldom seen in today's divorce-plagued society. Dad is the first man most little girls will ever love. From this father-daughter relationship, your little girl will establish her view of love. Dad, your daughter needs a hero, and guess what? She has chosen you. Friends, boyfriends, husbands, teachers, coaches, and professors will all influence her, but no one but Dad and Mom can shape her character and develop in her a foundational sense of security and self-worth. It doesn't matter if she is three years old or fifty-three years old: from your daughter's perspective, it's never too late to strengthen your relationship.

If dads knew how important they were to their daughters, most would be overwhelmed by the responsibility. Meg Meeker, M.D., in her book *Strong Fathers, Strong Daughters*, writes:

> I have watched daughters talk to fathers. When you come in the room, they change. Everything about them changes: their eyes, their mouths, their gestures, and their body language. Daughters are never lukewarm in the presence of their fathers. They might take their mothers for granted, but not you. They light up—or they cry. They watch you intensely. They hang on to your words. They hope for your attention, and they wait for it in frustration—or in despair. They need a gesture of approval, a nod of encouragement, or even simple eye contact to let them know you care and are willing to help.[1]

A dad's first role in his daughter's life is that of protector. A lot of this happens by just being available. When they are little, it is a simple matter of being present. When they get to be teens, boys enter the picture. I have made it clear to my daughters that I will interview every young man who asks to date them (more on this later). My oldest daughter had guy friends through high school, but very few of the boys her age pursued her as a girlfriend. My daughter is very beautiful, which I tell her often. When she wondered why she received less attention from the boys than some of her friends, I gave her two reasons. "One, you have a lot of self-confidence, and that can be intimidating to some boys. Two, you have a father who is very present and visible." Most young men are intimidated by the fact a girl's father is close. The boys knew they would be engaging in a relationship with me if they chose to engage with anything more than friendship with my daughter. Most young men are not secure enough for that, which affirms the fact that most are not mature enough for a relationship with a young woman in the first place.

In spite of the billions of dollars invested in media to mold your child's mind, you have the greatest potential influence. Don't give into the lie that you can't fight the influence of your child's peers if they start making wrong choices. The influence of movies, TV, magazines, music, the Internet, and computer games are very powerful. However, research supports that a father's love is the most important factor in keeping your young princess on the right path.

A note regarding TV viewing: I would encourage you not to put a TV in your child's room. Let TV viewing be a family activity so that you can choose together what to watch. Having a computer in the common room of the house is another safeguard against the dangers of Internet chat rooms and inappropriate sites. The world that our kids live in today is dangerous and dark. Open your eyes wide and see what she will face this week, this year, and in the next ten years.

I want to summarize a story from *Strong Fathers, Strong Daughters*. It is a story of a young girl from a small town, Ainsley, who went off to an Ivy League college. Ainsley's parents were naturally very proud of her accomplishment. Everything went well until her second year of college, when she started to make some poor choices regarding her social life. Her choices eventually got her kicked out of college. She had to make the painful phone call home to inform her parents of the situation. She dreaded facing them again because she knew how angry and disappointed they would be. It was a long, fretful trip home as she imagined the painful reunion of her mother crying and her dad screaming...or worse yet, silently shaming her as if she were never born. In spite of these fears, she knew she had to go home and face them.

When she finally arrived home, she saw her mother first. Her eyes were red from crying, and disappointment was visible all over her face. When Ainsley saw her father, to her surprise, he was strangely calm and kind, but still silent. Her mom didn't wait long and began shouting at her about how she wasted her life. She had shamed the family and destroyed her future. As Ainsley stood taking the verbal beating she had expected and anticipated, her father approached her. And what he did next Ainsley will never forget. He softly whispered, "Are you all right?" At this, she burst into tears. She knew her actions had hurt them, but she was also hurt, confused, and scared. Her father saw her pain and put his aside, knowing his little princess was in distress, and offered his love and protection. Her dad put aside his disappointment and chose not to focus on what others thought. He was there to help heal his hurting daughter. He became her hero that day like no other time. Ainsley tells this story like it happened yesterday, when it actually occurred more than thirty years earlier. In that moment, she learned it was not what she accomplished that he loved; he loved her, who she really was, deep down inside.[2]

Dads, you are your daughter's first love, and you lay your daughter's foundation of self-esteem and security. You are the place of safety that settles her stomach when she is facing really hard decisions. You will be the one she compares all other men in her life against. You can be her knight in shining armor if you choose.

The Lost Princess Found

Each night the "little princess from the kitchen" served the king his dessert and, just as she had done with the kitchen staff, she won over his heart as well. He told her that even after they found their lost princess, he would like her to stay near him in the palace. By the end of the third day, the line of little princesses had gone and the king and queen were forced to face the probability that their little princess had died during the revolt.

The king asked for Anna to come and sing to him and the queen, for they were saddened by the thought of not finding their little princess. The king knew Anna could heal some of the sadness of losing his own daughter. He had her sit on his lap while she sang one of her songs to lift his spirit.

After she finished her song, Anna returned to the kitchen, and just then the queen was called out to meet an important visitor to the palace. The queen almost fainted when she saw who the visitor was—standing just inside the palace door was Mina. The queen could still see her holding her little Anna in her arms that dreadful night seven years ago.

Mina timidly asked, "How is the little princess getting along?"

Perplexed by the question, the queen answered, "The princess has not been found. I fear she is dead."

"No, my queen," Mina said. "I brought the princess to the palace three days earlier to wait in line."

The queen immediately rushed Mina to the king and had her explain everything she did during the last seven years, raising and keeping the princess safe. Finally, Mina explained what the little princess looked like the day she was dropped off at the palace. The king turned to his servant and asked him the name of the kitchen girl who had served and sung to him the last three nights.

The servant replied, "Please don't think evil of us, my lord, but we all call her the little princess, for she won our hearts with her pure spirit and sweet character. She acts as a princess should in all that she says and does."

The king asked him to bring her to them as his heart lightened with anticipation. When she entered the room and saw Mina, she ran to her and threw her arms around her, holding her tightly. Mina held Anna's face in her hands and then reached around to lift up her brown curly hair to show the king and queen. As

Mina lifted the beautiful brown curls off Anna's neck, she revealed the precious, diamond-shaped birthmark. Tears of joy began to stream from everyone's eyes. The king once again held his little princess in his arms, the little girl whom he had fallen in love with during the last three days, and marveled that she was really his long-lost daughter.

After Anna learned the whole story and that her full name was Annacia Marie, she still liked Mina to call her Anna and everyone else in the palace to call her "little princess." Never before or after was there a princess so compassionate and kind. The king seldom let her out of his sight until the day she married a knight of noble character who had won her heart. But that story is for another time. And yes, they all lived happily ever after.

Application points:
- What did you learn from this chapter that you would like to implement?
- What words of encouragement would you like to say to your daughter?
- When would you like to begin saying them?
- If your daughter has no father present, what other positive male figures can speak into her life?

Chapter 8

Boys Becoming Knights

Little boys dream of being knights
then change their costumes.
Young men imagine themselves knights
then change their friends.
Common men think of knights
then change the channel.
Great men believe they are knights
then change the world.

—R.F.

My wife Carolyn and I hosted a birthday party for our twelve-year-old son. The theme of the party was the Middle Ages. As my son and his five invited friends entered our home, I informed them they were going to begin the party as pages and move on to being squires. I instructed them on the role of a page. I had them greet my wife formally and respectfully. They shared a meal of unsliced bread, a whole roasted chicken, buttered potatoes, ice cream, and a cake shaped like a castle. For the meal they were not allowed to use any utensils or napkins. Some of the boys dove right in and tore the bread and ripped apart the chicken. Others were more tentative and kept looking for places to wipe their hands.

While they ate, I read them a story of a young man who desired to become a knight. This young man went from being a page to a squire before finally, after much training and hard work, becoming a knight. It was a meal they will always remember.

For games, they rode on each other's backs in a pretend jousting competition. They practiced fencing with real fencing equipment. As the party came to a close, I gave them fake mustaches, and they all posed for pictures with the mustaches and their own swords they had brought from home.

The party was a great success, with just one major complaint. They didn't want to stop at pages and squires. They wanted to be knights. They asked if they would get to become knights by the end of the party. I told them that becoming knights would be for another day when they were older. It was encouraging to see their natural interest in becoming knights. It was my desire to help them see that becoming a knight was not a simple process but one that required discipline, hard work, and courage.

The modern conceptions of knights are rich with romantic and heroic imagery. The original historic concept of a knight carried no grand ideals; the word simply meant a mounted warrior. The word for *knight* in French is *chevalier*, Spanish—*caballero*, German—*Ritter*, but in all cases it simply means "horse-man." However, during the Middle Ages, knights took on a much more elevated position in society. The tales of noble deeds and powerful victories of knights in battle possess elements of fantasy.

It is, however, fantasy characters such as knights and Superman that ignite children's imaginations and motivate them to reach for greatness at a young age. As our children grow, they need more than fantasy to forge strong character and healthy morals. Mighty knights actually existed in history. These men stood out in society as heroes. Knights chose to uphold a code of conduct and standard far above common societies. The famous author Tennyson summarized the knightly code of conduct as: "Live pure, speak true, right wrong, follow the King."[1] Knights of the Middle Ages were far more than mounted soldiers; they were outstanding citizens, visionary leaders, and heroic protectors who set the example in character, morals, and deeds.

Most boys want to become knights but don't know how. The natural way for them to observe how to become a knight (or a man) is by observing their father or grandfather. Observation is the way most boys develop their concepts of manhood. Most of the questions stirring in the minds of young boys could be put to rest by a few meaningful conversations between father and son. The problem is that many men don't have a good idea of how to define masculinity or know what it means to be a man. In modern society, people all over the world are seeking to define and rediscover true masculinity. If fathers do not answer the question of what it means to be a man for their sons, sons are left to figure it out on their own.

An alarming number of households around the world are fatherless. Even in homes where fathers are present, communication between father and son needs to be intentional, not taken for granted. Our sons, if left to themselves, will construct their concept of manhood from other sources. Movies and television shows frequently depict men as clueless, with low morals, large muscles, and lots of money, or with some supernatural powers that are by chance or luck. The media's examples will lead our children down a road to failure. Young boys are full of questions. The chart below highlights what your son will hear from modern media and what they could learn from you.

Modern media often teaches that a real man:	Fathers can teach sons that a real man:
• must have big muscles	• lives courageously in life
• smokes and drinks	• leads others in integrity
• chases many women	• is faithful to his wife
• swears and fights	• is committed to his family
• drives fancy cars	• acts honestly and fairly
• works day and night at the office	• does his best using his talents
• never lets his guard down	• laughs and crys with passion
• holds his emotions inside.	• is committed to his friends.

Your son will form his concept of manhood somehow. If you as parents don't present timely answers to his questions, society and media will. Societies around the world, including your own, are all facing rising social problems (substance abuse, theft, rape, suicide, domestic violence, child abuse, prostitution, sexually transmitted diseases, and declining morals), which erode a nation's structural strength. There is a direct correlation between men and women's moral character and a nation's social stability. Nations are built on the backs of the morally responsible and reliable behavior of its citizens. Parents have the ability in one short span of fifteen to twenty years to instill in their children the character that will allow them to be productive, upright citizens (knights and princesses). Well-trained children will contribute to the order and success of a nation. A young man with a healthy view of his masculinity will be a blessing to others.

How can you answer if your child asks, "What is a real man?" Let me suggest five actions your son can develop to act as a man, one action for each finger on his hand. These five actions can help our children understand what it means to grow into manhood and involve him acting maturely, taking responsibility, walking with the wise, standing up for what's right, and behaving appropriately when no one is watching.

A Real Man:

1. **Puts childish ways behind him.** "When I was a child, I talked like a child, I thought like a child, I reasoned like a child. When I became a man, I put childish ways behind me" (1 Corinthians 13:11).

2. **Takes responsibility for his own actions.** "Live such good lives among the pagans that, though they accuse you of doing wrong, they may see your good deeds and glorify God on the day he visits us" (1 Peter 2:12).

3. **Walks with the wise and follows no fools.** "He who walks with the wise grows wise, but a companion of fools suffers harm" (Proverbs 13:20).

4. **Stands up for what is right and sets a good example.** "Don't let anyone look down on you because you are young, but set an example for the believers in speech, in life, in love, in faith and in purity" (1 Timothy 4:12).

5. **Behaves appropriately when no one else is watching.** "Serve wholeheartedly, as if you were serving the Lord, not men, because you know that the Lord will reward everyone for whatever good he does" (Ephesians 6:7–8).

These are five principles every parent can teach his son. They will help your child take concrete steps toward becoming a man of knightly character. In the following five chapters concerning knights, I will endeavor to give practical suggestions for helping you guide your son to understand what it means to be a man and a knight in a dark world. But now let me introduce the story of *The Knights of the Eastern Watchtower*.

The Knights of the Eastern Watchtower

Once upon a time, there was a kingdom with a wise and noble king. Most of his kingdom was peaceful and prosperous. However, in the far eastern section of his kingdom there were lands morally dark, merciless, and cruel. To protect the kingdom from the wickedness of the eastern lands, the king stationed Lord Renold, one of his wisest, most faithful knights, to serve as lord of the eastern watchtower.

The king charged Lord Renold with keeping watch and defending all those who lived in the borderlands from the wickedness of the east. His castle gave hope and stood as a single beam of sunshine in a land constantly threatened by clouds and darkness. Those seeking mercy and a better life lived near the castle and could flee inside when danger drew close.

Lord Renold led a band of strong and courageous knights. Renold himself was the son of a knight whose father was also a knight. His family history was filled with stories of heroism and valiant quests. The castle of the eastern watchtower also served as a place for training future knights. Young men who chose to turn from the wickedness of the land came and entered the castle as pages. They all hoped to prove themselves faithful and brave so that they would one day be knighted and join with Lord Renold and his knights in righting wrongs and fighting for justice.

One such page was Kleophis, who was brought to the castle by his parents. They saw in him the desire to stand up for truth and wanted to give him the opportunity to learn the ways of chivalry. So at the age of nine, Kleophis left his home and began serving as a page in the castle. His lessons were challenging, and his daily tasks were mundane and not at all as interesting as he had hoped. As a page, his duties involved taking care of the needs of the ladies of the castle as well as household chores and stable work.

One day while attending to his duties, he was asked to mop the floor in the Hall of Meetings. This was a great rectangular room with a large wooden table in the middle. The room was supported by large marble pillars and had beautifully painted murals on either side of the room. At the end of the table sat a large chair made of deep-colored redwood. Because of its size and craftsmanship, the chair looked more like a throne than a common chair. This was the place of honor for the lord of the castle to gather his knights for counsel before and after battles. The room was dimly lit by small torches hanging from the supporting pillars on either side of the room. But behind the lord's chair, a single beam of light shone from a high window and illuminated a shelf lined with large white stones. These stones were naturally irregular in shape, each about the size of a large cannon ball.

Kleophis couldn't help but stare at the stones, for though they were simply white in color, they seemed to glow from within rather than from the light shining through the window. Kleophis mopped his way around the large table until he stood directly in front of the shelf of stones. He so wanted to pick one up to test its weight and feel its texture, but didn't dare—he knew they were not meant to be handled. With the stones less than a foot away from his face, he could see names on some of the stones. They were not etched or painted with brush or pen, but the names shone from within the stones. Not all the stones had names, but just before Kleophis reached the end of the collection, he was startled by a noise right behind him. He was so surprised that he jumped and swung his mop around into a defensive position, as if it were a sword.

Kleophis was a sight to see, standing with his mop ready to attack the man who startled him. His appearance produced a deep and hearty laugh from Lord Renold, who had entered the room quietly and watched Kleophis as he studied each stone.

"What do you think of the stones?" his lord asked Kleophis.

As Kleophis prepared to answer, he was very thankful he had restrained himself from picking up a stone. "I have never seen anything like them— but whose names are these, and how do they appear from within the stones?"

To be continued at the end of each chapter...

Application points:

- What did you learn from this chapter that you would like to implement?
- What discussion about manhood would you like to have with your son?
- What activities can you plan together that would help him grow as a man?
- When would you like to begin?

Chapter 9

Training Knights for Greatness

Build me a son, O Lord, who will be strong enough to know when he is weak, and brave enough to face himself when he is afraid; one who will be proud and unbending in honest defeat, and humble and gentle in victory.

—Douglas MacArthur

I have always been fascinated by stories of bravery, especially stories relating back to medieval times when battles were fought on horses with sword and lance and champions emerged as a result of their skill and bravery. Most societies have stories of heroes who have become legends. Between the eighth and thirteenth centuries, Europe gave birth to numerous legends and romances. This era has entertained generations with stories of Charlemagne, Roland, Lancelot, and King Arthur with his Knights of the Round Table. It is understood that many of these stories are more fantasy than fact. But regardless of their historical accuracy, they have ignited hearts and inspired greatness in young lives around the world.

Most modern-day children's heroes acquire their power from outer space or genetic engineering; the knights of old were different. They went through rigorous training to develop their skill. Strength wasn't enough; they also needed to prove themselves kind, just, and brave before being considered great knights.

This chapter will focus on the historical rituals, vows, and disciplines that went into making a knight and the many useful parenting principles that can be gleaned from them. These principles can encourage our own children to reach new heights, to develop courage, to learn discipline, and ultimately, to live lives as noble men and women of character.

Sonnets, songs, and poems recorded much of what we know about this period of time. One of the most famous writers of this era was Geoffrey Chaucer. Chaucer was an English poet famous for his authentic and moving descriptions of knights in *The Canterbury Tales*. Chaucer's insights into the life of knights came firsthand since he served as a page at the court of

Elizabeth de Burgh, Countess of Ulster. Chaucer also saw knights in action as he served as a squire in Prince Lionel's company during the Hundred Years' War. He was captured in 1360 at the siege of Reims, but was later ransomed and spent the majority of the remainder of his life as part of the court. He was able to read Latin and French and distinguished himself as an exceptional writer. Like many of his time, he benefited greatly from his training as a page and squire, but was never knighted. Chaucer's training has added a depth to his writing that makes his prose come alive. Some argue that his knights popularized through literature are more fantasy than reality. However, like any great work of historical fiction, the true historical facts create credibility for a moving story and lead the reader to desire the world created by the author more than everyday reality.

One more fact worth noting is that the time in history in which knights emerged was one of the darkest ages recorded up to that point. In the midst of the Middle Ages, much of society had reverted to barbaric ways, living selfishly and seeking personal pleasure and worldly gain. It was in the midst of these dark times that noble characters arose.

The description of the Dark Ages seems to match many of the challenges that face our modern-day societies. Such challenging times call for modern-day knights to arise and show the way back to purity, truth, and righteous living.

Knights also excite young children because of how they looked and the weapons they used in defending justice. Powerful in their armor and mounted on a horse, their weapons, in addition to being useful, also had symbolism. The knight's sword was often looked at as a symbol of his calling. Legend surrounded a knight's sword. For example, Charlemagne carried Joyeuse, his knight Roland had Durendal, and King Arthur had Excalibur.

Boys are attracted to swords. One day I decided to test this theory regarding boys and weapons. I gave two boys sticks and timed them to see how long it took for them, with no instruction or prodding, to turn them into swords and begin sparring one another. What I found was that it literally took only seconds! This works with adults too. Strap a sword to a man's side and watch his posture improve. He will stand taller and walk with a bolder stride. There is a warrior deep within men that takes only a little encouragement to come out. The simple observable truth is that boys and men like toys, weapons, and tools. They use them to enhance their power. Men enlist tools in most of what they do. They lift hammers, put on helmets, and swing bats, golf clubs, and racquets.

In literature, a knight's armor developed symbolism through the knighting ceremony. In the French prose romance *Lancelot-Grail*, Arthurian knight Sir Lancelot was told by the Lady of the Lake the symbolic meaning of his armor. In her description, each piece of armor represents various aspects of his duty to the church as a Christian knight. The Lady of the Lake told him that his mail tunic protects his body, as he was to protect the church. His helmet guards his head as he should guard the church. In the same way his lance strikes fear into wicked men, so his own demonstration of power should keep enemies of the church at bay. His double-edge sword symbolizes that his service is to God and the people. Its sharp point symbolizes that the people must be obedient and follow his leadership. His horse was a symbol of Christian people who support him. In the same way that his horse supports him and follows his guidance, the Christian people support and follow knights.

The symbolism associated with a knight's armor and of becoming a knight highlights the noble role knights were expected to uphold during a very immoral time. It often seems that when hope is scarce and dark deeds reign, people search for beacons of light. Knights gave people hope by bringing order, civility, and truth.

Knights may be exciting and interesting, but how can we as parents help our sons develop knightly character? What can we do to teach our sons to become virtuous knights? Let me begin by listing some of the key actions we can teach in order to set our sons up for success. Here are seven steps:

1. **Create a bond with your son.** This can happen naturally in the early years as you spend quality time together.

2. **Model knightly character.** There is no substitute for setting a good example and modeling the behavior you desire to teach.

3. **Feed them a good diet of heroes.** Tell stories, read books together, watch movies that promote good values. Movies that show good guys standing up for what is right and fighting the bad guys.

4. **Create opportunities for them to serve others.** Examples include taking time to serve together at a food kitchen, helping a neighbor, or planning a family mission trip to help those in need.

5. **Reward knightly behavior.** Verbally praise your son when you see him acting chivalrous or kind.

6. **Celebrate his unique interests and talents.** Not all kids will like the athletic part of being a knight. Some may enjoy creating things like food or works of art. Whatever your son naturally enjoys, find the good in it and praise him.

7. **Schedule time to spend with your son.** There is no substitute for quality time— time for bonding, training, and just having fun.

The seventh step is of fundamental importance. Quality time is key in creating and maintaining a strong parent-child bond. Children naturally bond with parents and desire a close relationship. What will hinder the bond is when parents reject the relationship by being too busy. It is important to remember that time is one of our most valuable commodities. We are given only so many days to live and influence others by our actions on this earth. Many people are busy rushing while missing out on so many wonderful things happening all around them.

Let me briefly explain two types of time. One type of time is *chronos*. *Chronos* is a Greek word that is associated with time as exemplified by a calendar or clock. It is the root word from which we derive the words chronicle, chronology, and chronic. *Chronos* was a god in the Greek pantheon. He was a cruel minor god who cannibalized his own children and was always depicted as a glutton that was never satisfied. *Chronos* typifies the life of those who are driven. To *Chronos*, time was not a gift, but a thief that ate away life one bit at a time. It is easy, as parents, to view time in this way, with all the bills to pay, schedules to keep, and deadlines to meet.

The Greeks, however, had a second word for time: *kairos*. *Kairos* time was a gift given for a season. It represented the opportunity to do something fitting. *Kairos* time is not represented by twelve noon or any other specific time of day, month, or year; instead it is about asking, "What is this time for?" Ecclesiastes 3:1 has the same attitude: "There is a time for everything, and a season for every activity under heaven." As parents, we can see time in the *kairos* way. This will also help us view the short season of having our children under our roof as precious. This is a time given for life, love, learning, and growing. If we fail to embrace *kairos*, time will be gone and wasted, and our opportunity for positive influence will pass us by. Learning to seize the time given to us every day as a gift will help lead our children into a rich life.

The Chinese word for busyness is made up of two radicals, or characters. One is "heart," and the other is "killing." These two characters together create the word *busyness*. It is true that busyness is the slow killer of the heart. When our lives are too busy for a connection with our children at the heart level, we are just too busy.

> *I know that there is nothing better for men than to be happy*
> *and do good while they live. That everyone may eat and drink,*
> *and find satisfaction in all his toil—this is the gift of God.*
> —Ecclesiastes 3:12–13

One of the biggest life mistakes is that of being in a hurry. Being constantly rushed causes us to miss out on life's most important events. Life is full of activity that feeds our pride and starves our soul. Most of life's precious gifts can't be bought with cash—love, beauty, kindness, loyalty, and respect. All of life's most treasured gifts take time to cultivate, appreciate, and enjoy. Set aside time for listening, fun, and for reading stories to your son. Read stories of great knights and heroes who can inspire your sons to be knights of character in their school and among their friends.

> *Yesterday is history, tomorrow is a mystery, but today is a gift.*
> *That is why it is called the present.*
> —Oogway in *Kung Fu Panda* (2008)

The Meaning of the White Stones

Lord Renold explained that the white stones had been given to his father's father by a wise and holy man, who appeared following the first battle fought to free the village from a cruel and oppressing warlord. In the years following the battle, his grandfather built the watchtower and the portion of the castle where they now stood. Just before his grandfather's death, his name appeared on one of the stones. At that time, the same holy man again appeared and told the meaning of the name appearing on the stone: "When a knight proves himself to be of noble character, faithfully walking in bravery, purity, and humility while loving justice, his name will appear."

Lord Renold went on to explain that in the last three generations, only a dozen names had appeared on the stones. Most of the names appeared during the knights' last years or even after their deaths. These names and the lives they represented served as reminders for all knights to seek a higher path than that of the evil world surrounding the castle.

"To have one's name appear on a stone is the highest honor a knight of our order can receive because it is not gained by external accomplishments; it is a measure of the heart," said Lord Renold.

Kleophis served his days faithfully as a page and never forgot the words his lord shared with him that day. He also pestered the older knights to tell him about the lives represented by each name written on the stones. He thought so much about the former knights that he often seemed lost in thought. He would imagine the men, their battles, their victories, and the legacy they left behind. The lives they blessed, the battles they fought, and the inward discipline they practiced formed noble thoughts in his mind and heart.

Application points:

- What did you learn from this chapter that you would like to implement?
- What books or movies can inspire your son?
- What service or outreach projects can you plan with your son?
- When would you like to start?

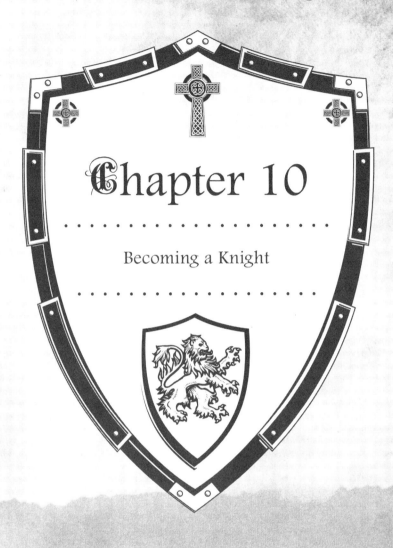

Chapter 10

Becoming a Knight

A true knight is fuller of bravery in the midst than in the beginning of danger.

—Sir Philip Sidney

William Marshal, a young man with courage and discipline, serves as an excellent historical example of how a boy could rise from humble origins to wealth and fame. Marshal, at one point, was so poor that he had to sell his clothes to buy a horse. In time, he rose so high in status that he was able to marry Isabel de Clare, heiress to Richard de Clare, Second Earl of Pembroke. She was one of the richest women in England. Let me briefly retell the story of this knight of humble origins and his rise to prominence in the world of chivalry.

At age thirteen, Marshal served as a squire at the court of his mother's cousin, William de Tancarville, Chamberlain of Normandy. Seven years later, he was knighted and joined the frontier war between King Henry II and the counts of Boulogne, Flanders, and Normandy. His youthful bravery almost cost him his life and did cost him his horse to his opponent. He was viewed as a hothead and was not given another horse, which was why he had to sell his clothes to buy one. From that point on, he steadily rose in reputation and wealth. He was brave in war, almost unbeatable at tournaments, and chivalrous. At the age of twenty-four, Marshal was appointed tutor in arms to the fifteen-year-old King Henry the Young. He was banished for one year because of rumored accusations of becoming too intimate with Margaret, the king's wife. He was reconciled to the king the next year, just before the king's death.

Following the king's funeral, Marshal went on a journey to the Holy Land because the dying king had given Marshal his cloak and made him promise to take it to Jerusalem. While in the Holy Land fulfilling his promise, Marshal made a solemn vow to be buried as a Templar Knight. The Knights of Templar were an order of warrior monks famous for protecting pilgrims on their way to Jerusalem and other holy places. They were established shortly after the first crusade around AD 1119. King Baldwin of Jerusalem allowed them to set up headquarters on the historic site of King Solomon's Temple. As a result, they became known as "The Knights of the Temple of King Solomon." Their name was later shortened to "Knights Templar." Saint Bernard de Clairvaux, one of their original patrons, wrote: "[A Templar Knight] is truly a fearless knight, and secure on every side, for his soul is protected by the armor of faith, just as his body is protected by the armor of steel. He is thus doubly-armed, and need fear neither demons nor men."[1]

The Knights Templar were an elite fighting force. Though relatively small in number, they joined larger armies. They were often used in the initial charge to break the enemy line. They fought alongside King Richard I of England and King Louis VII of France as well as in Spain, Portugal, and Palestine.

When Marshal returned from Jerusalem, he served King Henry II and fought in a campaign against the king's rebellious sons. During the fighting, Marshal isolated Prince Richard and could have killed him, but chose to kill only Richard's horse. Later, when Prince Richard became King of England, he honored Marshal for his kindness and offered the hand of Isabel de Clare, Heiress of Pembroke, one of the richest women in England.

Marshal's accomplishments include serving on the council of Regency while Richard I was away on crusades, being a signer of the Magna Carta, and, upon the King's death, being named Protector of the Kingdom. The Archbishop of Canterbury declared him "the greatest knight to have ever lived." With no royal bloodline, William Marshal serves as an excellent example of how a boy with a brave heart and noble character can change his world.

William Marshal followed the natural stages in becoming a knight. In most cases, a young boy pursuing knighthood would, at age seven or eight, move from his mother's home and reside in a castle as a page, living with the overlord or a relative. He would perform menial household duties for the queen or lady of the castle. Pages learned to serve and respect their lord and lady. By serving the lady of the castle, these boys became very aware of the respect and honor that is due to women. He learned about her needs and desires while serving her. In this way, he would later have insight that would allow him to rise above the barbaric marriages of the day based on a husband's physical domination of his wife. At this time he also learned about armor, weapons, and falconry while going about his duties. Pages received instruction and lessons from squires, minor clergy, priests, and traveling troubadours. A squire's instruction focused on many aspects of becoming a knight, such as horse riding and jousting at human-shaped dummies holding shields and rings.

At the age of fourteen, a page usually became a squire and was attached to a knight and accompanied him in all his travels. His duties were still to take care of the menial tasks of cooking and cleaning. He would carry the knight's armor as well as wake and dress him when such duties were requested. Life as a squire was not all serving though. In this season of life, he was allowed to compete in tournaments, so he was able to perfect his skill with the lance and sword. He learned to ride and improved his falconry. In these formative years, a squire was able to grow in strength and skill under the close eye and mentoring of his knight.

A knight's responsibilities were listed in the knight's code, which I mentioned earlier: "Live pure, speak true, right wrong, follow the King." His conduct was also defined by the concept of chivalry. Chivalry, much like filial piety within Chinese societies, was much more that just one single concept. It taught a young man how to behave in society and show proper respect to women of different ages. Young men need parameters in which to grow; these clearly defined ideals surrounding the concept of chivalry motivated young men to achieve increasing levels of excellence.

The title of knight brought with it a great amount of honor and responsibility. Not every squire became a knight, but they all strove to that end. Being dubbed a knight could be achieved in a few different ways. Some men were knighted before a great battle or before setting off on a crusade. Others were knighted following a battle in which they had proven themselves brave. In the latter part of the Middle Ages, squires could only be dubbed knights if they were sons of knights.

Think of what all this means for us as parents—not that we ship our kids off to a castle and let someone else train them as a page, squire, and knight! We are the most crucial people in helping our sons become knights. This model can inspire us to train our children to be of knightly character.

You may wonder why I don't talk about raising princes instead of knights. It is for the simple reason that only a few children born of a royal line were ever privileged with the responsibility of being a prince. They didn't have to work for it or achieve a high level of moral conduct to keep their title. Knights like William Marshal, on the other hand, were selected from men who from an early age disciplined themselves with the hopes of one day being dubbed a knight. This honor did not come easily or without much sacrifice. Knights went through some elaborate training. The most recognizable stages of becoming a knight were that of enlisting as a page, then advancing to squire, and finally, to the honor of a select few—being dubbed a knight.

Without transporting our children back to the Middle Ages, it is possible in our modern world to help our sons enjoy some of these knightly rites of passage. Many rite-of-passage ceremonies exist, but I will just highlight a couple of activities that I have enjoyed or plan to enjoy with my boys. When my boys were little, bonding happened quite naturally. We spent time wrestling together, throwing balls, or just hanging out around the home. I also read stories and talked to them about knights and regularly trained them in moral behavior. Shortly before puberty, usually between ages 11–13, I began talking more about what it meant to be a man. I also took a more active role in the lives of their friends, by helping lead their church youth group. Specific values and roles associated with the page stage were highlighted during our medieval-theme birthday party already described in Chapter 8.

Around this same time I took my son on an overnight retreat and talked about the changes he could expect at puberty. We also talked about sex, self-control, and how to treat girls with dignity. It was a great time to talk and agree on healthy boundaries regarding interacting with girls. We enjoyed using materials available through *FamilyLife* ministry called *Passport2Purity*.

These materials provided detailed instructions as well as suggestions for fun. This is definitely a father-son or mother-daughter event. In situations where a father or mother is not present, a trusted male role model for the sons and female role model for the daughters would also work.

When my son turned sixteen, I organized a special dinner for him where key men in his life came together. Each man shared words of encouragement and advice. This gathering was symbolic of beginning the squire stage. My son was invited into a community of men and began seeking formal and informal time with them as mentors and advisors.

The knight stage is still to come for me. It will likely happen following my son's graduation from college or when he becomes more financially independent from the home. As I look forward to this stage, I plan to hold a ceremony that involves affirmation as well as a gift. Robert Lewis and his ministry are an inspiration to me and they have many great materials for anyone seeking to raising young men.

Training our sons to become men of knightly character is a daily process and privilege. Specific ceremonies help us celebrate and acknowledge the growth and progress that is taking place. Ceremonies also let others join us as we celebrate our sons growing in knightly characteristics. With the help of others, our sons will grow in maturity as they grow in patience, kindness, courage, and self-control.

> *Better a patient man than a warrior, a man who controls his*
> *temper than one who takes a city.*
> —Proverbs 16:32

Kleophis Becomes a Knight

Over time, Kleophis advanced to serve as a squire. As a squire he was allowed to train and compete in tournaments, to his great delight. Kleophis wasn't the biggest or strongest young squire, but it seemed that he had the biggest heart and the strongest will. Watching him at sparring practice, you would have thought he was fighting for his life or saving a captive princess. His passion won him many friends and, unfortunately, one enemy.

Clue, a son of a wealthy knight, didn't like Kleophis stealing attention away from him, for Clue was accustomed to being first. He was taller and stronger than most of the squires, but he was also lazy. Things had come easy for Clue, and he seldom used his full energy when training in order to win. Kleophis, on the other hand, put every ounce of his muscle, his mind, and his sweat into each training exercise. Kleophis won some awards at tournaments, but his passion was what won him the admiration of his fellow squires and the knights in charge of training.

On the eve before an important competition, Clue played some very mean pranks on Kleophis. In the middle of the night, Clue poured pig oil and garbage from the kitchen on the floor in front of Kleophis's sleeping cot, making it a smelly, slippery mess. He then poured warm water over Kleophis's blanket and slipped out of the room. When the water seeped through his blanket, Kleophis awoke wet and cold. He threw the wet blanket off and jumped to his feet. As soon as his bare feet hit the oily floor, they slid out from under him. In one swift motion, he slipped, landed in the garbage, and banged his head on his cot. He immediately knew it was the work of Clue, knowledge confirmed by Clue's loud laughter just outside the door and the scuffle of his feet running from the scene. Cold and angry, he could not get back to sleep and instead lay in bed thinking of ways to get back at Clue.

Kleophis dressed early for the competition and made his way to the field. Clue knew Kleophis would be angry and that anger often made people careless when fighting, so he chose him as his first opponent in the wooden sword competition. Kleophis was indeed angry and not thinking clearly as he prepared to face Clue. However, just before the match began, Kleophis remembered the words of one of the great knights in the castle: "Better is the man who controls his temper than one who takes a city."

Kleophis took these words to heart and let go of his anger. The competition began, and Clue found he was evenly matched by Kleophis's strategic fighting style. Kleophis's cool head and swift moves forced Clue to fight with his full strength for the first time, just to keep from being beaten. In the end, the match was ruled a draw, but during the match Clue received many painful blows from Kleophis's sword. Clue was amazed at Kleophis's ability to overlook his *insults and practical jokes. That day Clue learned to respect Kleophis, and he was challenged to work harder himself.*

Just before a great battle in the northeastern border of the kingdom, Kleophis's hard work was rewarded, and he was dubbed a knight of the eastern watchtower. In his very first battle, he proved himself brave. When his company of knights was driven back, he alone stood his ground until other knights led by Clue returned and joined him. At another crucial point in the battle, Kleophis stood over Clue, who had fallen after being struck in the calf by an archer's arrow. While standing over Clue, he struck the enemies' armor with such force that his own sword broke in two, so he used Clue's sword until the battle was won.

Application points:
- What did you learn from this chapter that you would like to implement?
- What rite-of-passage ceremony can you plan for your son? Visit our website at www.summituniversitymedia.com for rite-of-passage ideas.
- When would you like to begin carrying out your plan?

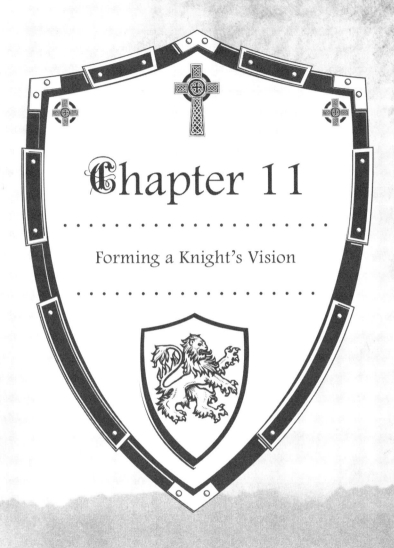

Chapter 11

· ·

Forming a Knight's Vision

· ·

*The most pathetic person in the world is
someone who has sight, but has no vision.*

—Helen Keller

Literary descriptions of knights were a crucial element in the development of a young squire's vision. Each stage of becoming a knight was meant to teach and instruct their heart and mind.

Young men could achieve knighthood via a few different paths, but once a squire was selected to become a knight, he needed to perform certain assignments or ceremonies as part of the process. These ceremonies were filled with symbolism and religious meaning. *The Book of Chivalry* gives a description of the knighting ceremony. The squire first would take a bath one day before his knighting ceremony, symbolizing washing away his sins and emerging with a clean conscience. He would then rest in a bed made with white sheets, symbolizing the peace one feels when they have a cleansed conscience resulting from God's forgiveness. He then dressed in new white clothes and a scarlet robe. The white clothes symbolized new virtue, while the robe reminded him that he must be willing to shed his own blood in defense of Christianity and the church. To remind him to turn away from pride and vainglory, he wore black socks, symbolizing the earth. He came from dust and to dust he would return, and he would not know the hour of his death. He also wore a white girdle for chastity.

Once he was dressed, he kept vigil that night to remind him that evil does not sleep and he must be always watchful for it. During the actual knighting ceremony, he was given a golden spur. Gold represented the most coveted metal. It was worn on his foot, the farthest point from his head and heart. He was given a sword to defend justice and reason. Finally, he received a kiss from a knight, representing loyalty and love. Then the same knight would strike him on his shoulder. This blow to his shoulder was to help him never forget that now he was a knight and must from this day forward uphold the laws of chivalry.

The Chivalry Code emphasized that a knight's virtues mattered far more than his wealth and possessions. However, good knights would acquire worldly wealth as a result of their faithful service and heroic deeds. The Code also expected a knight to win the love of a woman by showing himself worthy and faithful to the woman he loved.

For example, Sir Galahad, one of the Arthurian knights, was a very spiritual knight. His tales emphasized how he was humble, innocent, and pure. Alfred Tennyson describes one of the knights's visions in a poem titled *Sir Galahad*, published in 1842:

> *My good blade carves the casques of men,*
> *My tough lance thrusteth sure,*
> *My strength is as the strength of ten*
> *Because my heart is pure.*

Tennyson continues by talking of heaven, light, and peace:

> *A maiden knight—to me is given*
> *Such hope, I know not fear;*
> *I yearn to breathe the airs of heaven*
> *That often meet me here.*
> *I muse on joy that will not cease,*
> *Pure spaces clothed in living beams,*
> *Pure lilies of eternal peace,*
> *Whose odours haunt my dreams.*[1]

Sir Galahad was remembered for his deeds at arms as well as his religious faith, wisdom, and generosity.

King Edward I of England stands out in history's record as a man of vision and for his loving devotion to his wife. Edward was first knighted by King Alphonso X of Castile at the age of fifteen. This knighting took place just before his marriage to King Alphonso's thirteen-year-old half sister Eleanor on November 1, 1254. At age twenty, he was already proving his strategic sense and military prowess. While in battle, news reached him that his father, King Henry III, had died. At that time, he signed a treaty and returned to England, where he was crowned King Edward I.

Edward was also remembered for his care of his wife Eleanor of Castile. She would often travel with him and even accompanied him on crusades. He was also devoted to the Christian church. He founded Vale Royal Abbey in 1277 in Cheshire. He purportedly did this to fulfill a vow he made to build an abbey for the Cistercian monks after he survived a shipwreck during a crossing of the English Channel in 1263–64. When it was believed that the bodies of Arthur and Guinevere were found at Glastonbury, he reinterred them at the Glastonbury Abbey in 1278.

His devotion to his lady and the church was complemented by his interest in Arthurian tradition. To celebrate conquering Wales, he held an Arthurian "Round Table" at Nefyn in Wales in 1284. From 1279 to 1302, he resided over several Arthurian Round Tables at Kenilworth, Warwick, and Falkirk. As a man, he was physically imposing. Standing six feet, two inches, which was extremely tall in thirteenth-century England, he had thick curly hair and was nicknamed "Longshanks." When he wasn't at war or embarking on crusades, he enjoyed hunting and hawking. King Edward I stands out as a knight with a vision for his country, faith, and lady. His example further strengthened young men of his time to live as knights.

King Edward's example can encourage us to teach our sons to:

1. **Develop a vision for their country by taking responsibility for the world around them.** We need to teach our sons to stand up for what is right and be faithful and loyal to their friends. By living generously with their time, talents, and money, they can serve others as knights.

2. **Cultivate a vision for their faith by developing a personal relationship with God through Jesus Christ.** Young men should not ignore their spiritual growth and development. A relationship with God can strengthen a young man's values and moral conviction. Their spiritual growth should result in a closer relationship with God as well as a better relationship with others.

3. **Understand what it looks like to have a vision for their lady.** This can be accomplished by teaching that there is a wonderful young lady out there for them to love. They need learn to be worthy of her love by living pure and respectable lives.

Knights of old acted in a way that earned the respect of other men as well as the admiration of women. Women today still look for their knight in shining armor. Our sons can be challenged to be pure men in thought and deed who will become some maiden's knight in shining armor. Most boys in their teen years want to be noticed and liked by girls. We can encourage our sons that by staying pure and behaving as a knight, they will eventually be attractive to girls of character. Young people can be shown a picture of marriage as something wonderful and worthy of sacrifice. Young men of every age need a compelling vision in order to stay pure before marriage. We can teach that purity will result in a more wonderful and sexually fulfilling marriage in the future. With a compelling vision to win the heart of the women they love, our knights can learn to resist temptations.

I have challenged my son to walk in purity and enlist the strength of friends in order to strengthen his resolve. He has created accountability partners who, along with himself, desire to keep themselves sexually pure until they marry the women they love.

It's important that your son has a clear vision and accountability to support him in staying pure. As our story *Knights of the Eastern Watchtower* continues, Kleophis needs to remember his compelling vision in order to overcome a very tempting situation.

The Battle for Purity

Kleophis's bravery at such a young age was the talk of the village. The story was told from house to house of how he had stood his ground in battle defending the fallen knight. He was the pride of his parents and soon became the heartthrob of many young maidens in the village.

One evening as he was returning to the castle from visiting his parents, he passed a group of young men and ladies telling stories and laughing among themselves. When they spotted Kleophis, they begged him to join them and tell of his tales in battle. His stories, appearance, and reputation drew the attention of all the young ladies present. They left the street and entered a home of one of the young ladies.

While telling his stories, he was especially aware of one beautiful girl sitting across from him. She wasn't dressed as modestly as the ladies of the castle, and she seemed very free in showing her interest toward Kleophis. She was certainly beautiful, and as the night grew late, most of the guests left. Soon it was just the two of them alone in the home. He had heard her share earlier to her friends that her parents were away and were not expected home until the next day. Her beauty and flirtatiousness made it difficult for him to think of anything else. He was tired of all the rules of the castle and his hard training. It was natural for him to take a break and enjoy spending time with young people in the town.

As he was thinking these thoughts, he was startled by a door slamming from a gust of wind. The last guest had forgotten to properly close it. The loud noise woke Kleophis from his stupor, giving him a moment of clarity. He realized his passion was stirred, and his mind told him why his moral standards were not reasonable. Compromise was filling his thoughts. He knew of only one brave way to fight this moral battle. All at once, he did what every brave noble knight should do in such a situation.

Without giving reason for his departure, he turned and ran—in fact he ran all the way back to the castle. Once safely inside, he shared his struggle with an older knight, who praised him for his swift feet as well as exhorted him to avoid compromising situations like that in the future. Kleophis had won his second great battle that month and had learned that the best way to win some battles is to flee.

Application points:

- What did you learn from this chapter that you would like to implement?
- When will you talk to your son about purity and its importance?
- What accountability can you set up for your son to strengthen his fight for purity?
- What activities can you encourage to help your son develop a strong faith?

Chapter 12

A Knight's Quest

It's what you do that defines you.
—Batman in *Batman Begins* (2005)

Knights in the Middle Ages accepted the challenge of going on quests to prove their strength and bravery. It is interesting how modern men find ways to turn everyday life into quests. Without realizing it, I seem to make every opportunity for long-distance travel into a challenge to conquer. I find out how long it should take to get there. I attempt to limit bathroom stops and encourage the kids not to drink too much so we can stop less. My wife—and likely most rational women in the world—thinks this is crazy. When I travel alone or with my teenage son, we attack a road trip. If we encounter danger along the way in the form of hailstorms, snowstorms, or other hazards, it just adds to our tale of how we made it through. In general, the male species is made for action. Men, by their very nature, like to relate to the world through physical interaction. Men do. When they are not doing, they are usually talking about doing or others who are doing. Men are made for action.

Knights were symbols of true masculinity, men using their strength and ability to do what is right. The knights-errant set out on adventures to prove their bravery and chivalry. These missions involved freeing besieged castles or bringing order to troubled lands. It was also, at times, to save damsels in distress.

Boniface of Montferrat was famous for such chivalric exploits. He resided over the court in northwest Italy during the late twelfth and early thirteenth century. His court was one of the most chivalrous courts in all of Europe. Boniface became the topic of many songs and poems. On one adventure, he rescued Saldina de Mar of Genoa. She had been kidnapped by Albert of Malaspina and was held captive in his stronghold. As the story goes, Boniface and Raimbaut, a fellow knight, rode straight in during the evening meal and rescued her, then delivered her safely to her lover, Ponset d'Aguilar.

The Epic Letter tells of another lady rescued by Boniface. Lady Jacobina of Ventimiglia was being held by her wicked uncle, Count Otto. He was planning to take her money and send her away to Sardinia. When Boniface heard of Lady Jacobina's situation, he remembered an earlier encounter with Jacobina where she had kissed him and asked him to protect her from her evil, scheming uncle. Boniface and Raimbaut once again rode out, along with Bertoldo, Guiot, and Hugonet del Far. These five knights rode by night and rescued her from her ruthless uncle Count Otto only moments before she was to be sent into exile.

Once Lady Jacobina was out of her uncle's fortress, they still faced many dangers and were pursued by many enemy knights in the service of Count Otto before they reached safe lands. Many things were against them. They were greatly outnumbered, and they went without food and water for two days. In one of their battles, Raimbaut was wounded and would have perished if not for the aid of Bertoldo and Hugonet del Far. That night, they found shelter in the home of Sir Aicio, who was so impressed by the virtue, appearance, and reputation of Boniface that he offered his beautiful daughter, Aigleta, to him as his bride. Boniface chose to decline his offer, but arranged wonderful marriages for both Aigleta and Jacobina. Once Jacobina was safe, he ensured that her inheritance was restored.

His loyal companion Raimbaut boasted of Boniface's reputation in courtly love. He had arranged at least one hundred marriages for ladies without the proper means to secure good matches, providing them loving husbands from among noble barons, marquises, and counts. However, Boniface had never given into the temptation of taking advantage of these ladies in need of his help. His exploits included unseating enemy knights on the field, attacking castles, climbing sheer walls, and leading the fourth crusade. Boniface's actions and character set a wonderful example for younger squires and knights.

I was recently honored to speak at a Boy Scouts' award ceremony. A young man that grew up in our church, and who is a close friend and accountability partner of my teenage son Timothy, was receiving his Eagle Scout award—the highest honor awarded to a Boy Scout. I was impressed by all the codes of conduct that were emphasized for these young men, but one code stood out in particular. During the presentation, he recited that a Boy Scout was to do a good deed for someone else every day. Think about the effect of this habit on a family, society, or school. Young men everywhere would be seeking opportunities to help people every day. Such an ideal, when lived out, would certainly create an outstanding citizen whom others would enjoy being around. This sounds a little like young men performing knightly acts of chivalry.

> *On my honor I will do my best*
> *To do my duty to God and my country*
> *and to obey the Scout Law;*
> *To help other people at all times;*
> *To keep myself physically strong,*
> *mentally awake, and morally straight.*
> —Boy Scout Oath

Most men choose a quest—some are of noble pursuit and others less so. For example, many men dream of being a man-child, escaping all unwanted obligations of the adult life. They dream of living free of burdensome responsibilities with time at their disposal, lacking nothing but the ability to pursue the desire for happiness and fulfillment. This type of dream becomes an obsession for many and causes them to fall into "get rich quick" businesses. I'm all for dreaming and for taking appropriate risks, but not for the purpose of escaping. An ambition of a leisurely, challenge-free life is a far cry from a knight righting wrongs and making the world better. These are small ambitions with little personal reward and even less blessings for others. If we, as parents, are guilty of these pursuits, children will likely set their personal ambitions equally low.

Most boys would find taking a quest very exciting, envisioning themselves performing heroic deeds and saving the day. But what does a quest in the twenty-first century look like? Those in distress are more likely to be fellow classmates or elderly people living in our neighborhoods than damsels trapped in faraway castles. The circumstances are different, but these people need our assistance in similar ways that damsels in distress did in years past. Helping our children see this connection may be accomplished by asking them some basic questions such as:

1. Have you ever seen other kids or adults in a distressed situation?
2. Who were they, and what was the situation?
3. Can you think of any way in which someone could have helped them?
4. What would it look like if you were the one to help them?
5. How would that person feel when you helped them out of their trouble?
6. What danger would you face by being the person to come to their rescue?

Your children may quickly point out the danger of embarrassment and rejection. Instead of being cut with swords, your kids are in danger of being hurt by a peer's cutting comment. Your son may not be shot at with arrows, but people can shoot him with questioning or angry looks. These dangers are very real, and only one with knightly character will choose to do good in the midst of such dangers.

Peer pressure is a powerful force that leads many young people down the wrong path. Teaching our children to overcome peer pressure and stand true to what is right is a regular challenge for adults. I can remember getting in trouble as a child for breaking a rule and saying to my mom, "All the other kids were doing it." She would reply with the classic answers, "Just because they were all doing it doesn't make it right," and "If they were all jumping off the bridge, would you follow?" My answer should have been no, but I am sure I thought it depended on how high the bridge was. Nevertheless, I understood the principle of learning to do what was right even when others were acting differently. Learning this lesson in my early adolescence made a big difference when I entered junior high and high school. By choosing to stay true to the values I was taught, I avoided a lot of trouble and helped some of my friends avoid trouble as well.

Every quest is unique, and our children's quest will look very different from what Boniface and his brave companions faced. However different our worlds may be, our modern society is filled with those in distress and in need of valiant knights.

As our story continues, Kleophis faces a test of competing desires. What he does not realize is that making the right choice is a matter of life or death.

The Test of Commitment

Kleophis was well received by his fellow knights and enjoyed training and the camaraderie of all in the castle. At the same time, he was eager to fight more battles and further prove his bravery. The lands surrounding the eastern watchtower were enjoying a well-needed time of peace. No raiding parties were attacking the outer villages. No enemy lands were seeking to invade their territory. Lord Renold encouraged his knights to continue to train and be prepared. He exhorted them, "Do not become lazy in times of peace, or we will be found unprepared if war should break upon us."

Kleophis respected his lord, but inwardly wished Lord Renold would send him on a knight's errand to a land in need of a brave knight such as himself.

As fate would have it, the kingdom on the other side of the eastern ridge of mountains was struggling against bands of raiders from the dark northern forests. This was just the type of fight Kleophis hoped for. A request came to the lord, asking for his assistance in controlling the raiders. However, when Lord Renold listed the knights whom he would send, Kleophis was not among them. He was asked to stay with the remnant of knights at the castle. This was a major disappointment to Kleophis, who inwardly felt he deserved to go because he had proven himself brave in the last battle. A group of knights his own age were also very disappointed in not being allowed to go and fight. They came up with a plan to sneak off and join the fight, in spite of their lord's wishes for them to stay back. Kleophis was excited by this plan and packed and prepared for the secret departure the next day.

As he lay in bed that evening thinking of the adventure he would surely enjoy, his conscience became troubled. For he remembered the oath he had taken to obey his lord and faithfully serve under his leadership. He began to see that his plan to sneak off to battle (noble as it sounded) would be breaking his oath to obey and serve faithfully. To keep his oath "even when it hurt" meant not just in battle against enemies, but also fighting battles against boredom. His faithfulness needed to prove itself through perseverance. After he awoke the next morning, he shared his convictions with the other young knights and challenged them to reconsider their plan.

In the end, they all stayed at the castle, and it was a good thing too, for shortly after the selected knights left to fight the raiders beyond the eastern ridge, another group of raiders attacked a village within their own borders. All the knights remaining in the castle were needed to drive them away and save the village. Kleophis fought the battle with steadfastness, and the villagers were lucky that he had won his inner battle. For without the group of younger knights, their battle would have been lost.

Application points:

- What did you learn from this chapter that you would like to implement?
- Ask your son the questions listed in this chapter, and help him create a modern quest.
- Discuss with your son the importance of overcoming pure pressure and doing what you know is right.
- When would you like to begin?

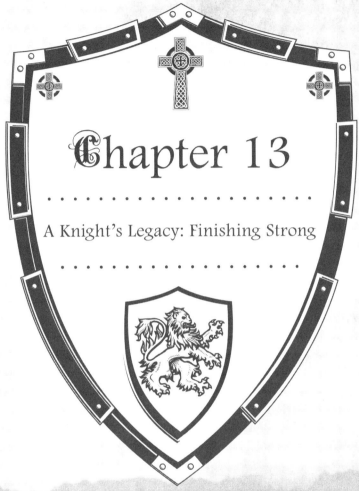

Chapter 13

. . . .

A Knight's Legacy: Finishing Strong

. . . .

And Lord knows, kids like Henry need a hero—courageous, self-sacrificing people setting examples for all of us. Everybody loves a hero. People line up for them...cheer them...scream their names. And years later, they'll tell how they stood in the rain for hours just to get a glimpse of the one who taught them to hold on a second longer. I believe there's a hero in all of us...that keeps us honest...gives us strength...makes us noble...and finally allows us to die with pride...

—Aunt May in *Spider-Man 2* (2004)

As parents, one of our goals is teaching our children how to finish strong. Beginning well is important, but finishing strong is equally important. There are knights who finished strong and as a result left a legacy. It is almost impossible when discussing knights and chivalry to leave out King Arthur. King Arthur represents the chief hero of the era of knights. Many modern historians believe that the legends of King Arthur are exaggerated accounts of a Welsh prince of the fifth and sixth centuries. This prince led a united British resistance against the invading Saxons.

One of the most celebrated victories was believed to have occurred at Mount Badon in AD 500. According to *History of the Britons*, Arthur fought the Saxons in at least twelve battles, and it also mentions the great victory at Mount Badon (an account also found in the *Annals of Wales*). His life might be exaggerated, but it is exciting to learn that he actually lived and was a great leader.

In the eleventh century, Geoffrey of Monmouth recorded the Arthurian legend in his *History of the Kings of Britain*. In this account, Arthur became king when the country was being attacked by Saxons. He drove them back and then married the beautiful Guinevere. His rule marked the golden era of chivalry, and he established the magnificent city of Camelot at the center of his kingdom.

The legend developed further in the thirteenth century in French romances, which added that Arthur was destined from birth to become king. A magical sword, Excalibur, was frozen in a stone. The inscription on the stone stated that only the true king of England could remove the sword. Many strong and noble knights tried to pull the sword from the stone, but none were able to move it. That is, until Arthur happened to visit London as a lowly squire. A great tournament was being held in London, and the winner would be chosen to lead the country. This was their own solution for leadership, since none were able to remove the sword from the stone. When Arthur, serving as a squire for his half brother Kay, forgot his brother's sword, he saw the sword in the stone and pulled it out. He then took the sword to Kay, who tried to claim that he pulled it from the stone. The noble knights saw through Kay's lie and confirmed that Arthur had done it. This supposedly accidental incident revealed him as the destined king and deliverer of Britain. In the fifteenth century, the knight Sir Thomas Malory made the legends available in English. Little changed between Geoffrey of Monmouth's twelfth-century legend and Sir Thomas Malory's fifteenth-century English version, with the exception of being the development of chivalry and the knighthood.

Arthur grew into more than a warrior and became a leader of the Knights of the Round Table. He stood for more than brute strength and was remembered as a great leader of men and a man of principle who believed in sharing power and authority with his fellow knights. His bravery won battles, but it was his humility and philosophy of leadership that made him such a great figure of legend and inspiration.

It was a great honor for a knight who finished well to be included in a story, poem, or song. To be written into one of these meant the knight had done something worth remembering. Knights were inspired by such stories to act bravely, to stand up for the weak, and to show kindness. Things haven't changed much in the minds of young people during the last six hundred years.

Just recently, my children were talking about playing a small part in a movie. Their part would be to play Westerners caught by the Japanese in China and interned in a concentration camp during World War II. My children's response to the opportunity was, "It would be so cool to see our names in the credits." My kids are expressing a very natural desire for recognition. The thought of doing something that will be recorded in a way that you can show others comes naturally.

Humility is a trait that helps people finish strong. Arthur's concept of sharing leadership with fellow knights showed real humility. This concept was repeated when knights were asked to participate in leading the first parliament. A knight's role in society involved more than just guarding against foreign enemies. He also served as a keeper of the peace and had the general duty of providing safety for widows, children, and others needing protection. The order of the Knights Templar, in particular, offered protection to those making pilgrimages to Jerusalem and other holy lands. In the thirteenth century, two knights from each county were summoned to attend a government council. This council, established by the English nobleman Simon de Montfort, served as a precursor to the modern parliament. King Edward I called a representative council referred to by historians as the Model Parliament because it was the first English representative government. This meeting was later called Parliament, as it is derived from the French word *parlement*, a "talk." This Model Parliament included many diverse representatives—magnates, churchmen, representatives of the lesser clergy, two burgesses from each borough, two citizens from each city, and two knights from each county.

The most lasting, and arguably the most important, thing a knight accomplished was to see that his children grew into knights. Young boys naturally follow their fathers. However, fathers who choose alcoholism, immorality, or are absent can destroy this natural instinct.

In the latter part of the Middle Ages, the northeast kingdom of Spain issued a legal decree from the Cortes of Catalonia, which read: "We decree that no one shall be knighted unless he is a knight's son." The same could be said in our day. If we hope to successfully train our sons to be men of knightly character, fathers, grandfathers, or mentors must first be men of knightly character. They must finish well in order for their life testimony to leave a positive legacy. It takes a knight to sire a knight.

I remember the time in high school when my father taught me about finishing strong. My brother and I were working on a landscaping job. Digging holes and planting flowers all day wasn't a lot of fun, but we learned how to work hard and the money was always appreciated. After a long day in the hot sun, we were always anxious to finish. Once most of the job site was clean, we were tempted to leave it. My dad, however, wouldn't let us leave until all the scraps and dirt in hard-to-see places were cleaned up. When everything was clean and left better than we found it, we could leave. He often said the difference between professionals and amateurs is how they finish a job. Finishing strong was something that can be emphasized in sports, work, relationships, and all of life.

I don't know about you, but I have a desire, a hope, or maybe it's just a dream, to see the rise of modern-age chivalrous knights. I also believe this dream lives in the hearts of modern-day maidens who are waiting for their knight in shining armor. It lives in every boy who turns a stick into a sword. It lives in the heart of men who desire the respect and admiration of their peers. It lives in the hearts of husbands who want to be the protecting hero for their wives and children. It may be sleeping dormant in the inner heart, but like anything that sleeps, it can be awakened.

Will you fathers, uncles, grandfathers, friends take the time and energy to awaken the knight within you and lead the next generation into chivalrous knighthood? Will you mothers find men of knightly character to lead your sons? Will you lead by example and show young men what it looks like to walk in humility and finish strong? I believe this dream of modern-age chivalrous knights can come true. The choice is ours.

The fear of the LORD teaches a man wisdom,
and humility comes before honor.
—Proverbs 15:33

The Temptation of Pride

Kleophis, in his middle age, had distinguished himself as one of the bravest, strongest, and most faithful knights in the castle. Even though he was twice the age of the younger knights, his strength and skill had no equal. He regularly sparred with the young knights in training, challenging two or three at one time just to keep it interesting. These sparring matches came with the occasional injury and wound, and one day he was a little overconfident and took on four young knights who, with great difficulty, bested him. He wasn't seriously injured, but his leg was severely bruised.

At the same time, a great battle broke out in the neighboring kingdom, and Lord Renold and his men were called for. All the knights prepared their armor and weapons for battle. In the great hall of the stones, the lord handed the gate key to Kleophis and asked him to guard the gate until they returned. Kleophis looked perplexed and asked respectfully why he would not be going to the battle. Surely one of the younger knights could guard the gate. Though he was slightly wounded from training, he was still stronger and more skilled than all but a few of the strongest knights. Lord Renold would not change his mind, and Kleophis watched as the knights rode out in shining armor ready for adventure. The lord stopped as he passed Kleophis and instructed him to keep watch guarding the gate and let no one enter until he himself returned.

A long time passed after the knights left the castle. Watching the gate left Kleophis time to struggle with his thoughts. He wondered if maybe he had become too old. Did Lord Renold think he was no longer strong enough to fight? Were his days of glory and battle past him? Late in the evening, just before dusk, a single knight approached the drawbridge leading up to the castle gate. He was clearly wounded and dressed in the colors of their allies. He called to Kleophis, saying he had a message from the battlefront.

"Speak your message. Tell me of the battle," Kleophis shouted back.

The knight reported, "The battle goes poorly. Our knights are being pushed back. Your lord asked me to look for more reinforcements. I see that you are an old knight. Are there any young, stronger knights who can come to the aid of their fellows?"

These words struck at Kleophis's heart and pride, for he knew he was stronger than most knights half his age. But he also knew he had sworn to guard the gate. He replied to the knight that no knights remained in the castle and he could not go, for he had sworn to guard the gate.

The wounded knight replied, "Convenient that you have such an excuse to stay out of battle, for it is very dangerous. Let me come and rest a while in the castle, and then I will be on my way."

Kleophis, burning with anger at these words, knew the knight was mocking him and calling him a coward. In spite of his wounded pride, Kleophis followed his lord's orders and did not let him enter the castle.

When the knight saw that he could not enter the castle, he rode off into the woods. From the top of the wall, the townspeople could see what Kleophis could not see—the wounded knight was actually an enemy, and a band of rogue knights waited in the woods ready to rush into the castle once the gate opened.

Less than an hour passed, and Kleophis heard a bugle blast signaling a victory. Lord Renold returned and was greeted by Kleophis as he passed through the gate into the castle. Once inside, the knights took their seats in the hall of meeting. Kleophis reported that all was calm while they were gone and only one wounded knight returned to seek further support for the battle. He walked past the stones on the shelf and presented the key to the gate back to the lord. On his way back to his seat, all the knights rose and looked past their seated lord to the shelf of stones. One stone began to illuminate the room as Kleophis passed it. On closer inspection, they all saw Kleophis's name appear on the stone.

All eyes turned to Kleophis to learn of what heroic deed he must have performed that day for him to be honored so. Astonished as the rest, Kleophis had no reply.

In the midst of the silent stares, Lord Renold spoke. "Men look at outward appearances, but the Lord of the stones is able to see our hearts as well as our deeds. Kleophis must have won a battle today at the gate that took greater courage than what we faced on the field."

Later, people from the town shared the story of the enemy knights in the woods. Kleophis had won a great battle that day and saved many lives; he had won the battle against pride.

At the time of Lord Renold's death, his name also appeared on one of the stones. He and Kleophis were the only two knights of their generation to receive names on the stones.

The stories and further deeds of Kleophis are recorded in the annals of the knights of the eastern watchtower. They serve as a reminder to young men who want to be great knights that the greatest battles to be won will be of the heart and will.

Application points:

- What did you learn from this chapter that you would like to implement?
- How can you teach your son to finish strong?
- What steps are you taking to ensure that you finish strong and leave behind a legacy?
- What can you do or plan today in order to sire your knight?

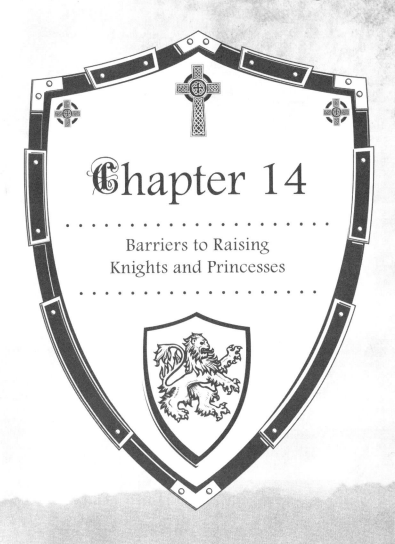

Chapter 14

· ·

Barriers to Raising
Knights and Princesses

· ·

Plans fail for lack of counsel,
but with many advisers they succeed.

—Proverbs 15:11

Does parenting seem like waging war to you? It does in our home at times. When waging a war, strong leaders seek counsel. In the same way, parents and grandparents should seek all the wise counsel they can find.

Recently, I was talking with a friend of mine who is building an addition on his house. He is from Australia, but currently lives in a small country town in Mongolia. As a result of his remote location, he has to do most of the work himself. As we talked, he said he was about to lay the first layer of blocks. The first layer is always the most important because it acts as the foundation. If they are not straight, the entire wall will not go up straight. He said he was going to start laying the blocks yesterday, but decided to wait until today when a professional builder was able to come over and help. He was wise enough to realize that when it comes to foundations, we should seek the best advisors possible.

The same holds true when we are talking about building foundations for our children's lives. Their future is too important for us to rely only on our own wisdom. Rather, we should seek all the advice and help we can get. No one will be more influential than you in building your child's foundations. Because of this, you should seek wise council frequently and whenever possible.

I want to discuss some attitudes that will prevent you from improving your parenting—attitudes that will stop you from making a thorough diagnosis of your child's needs and your current parenting practices. The most common barriers hindering parents from effective parenting are:

- overcompensating
- being fearful

- being overly defensive
- underestimating human depravity
- overdelegating.[1]

By overcoming these common barriers, you will clear the way for your children to be trained by the most appropriate child trainer in their world—you. Let's begin by facing our personal obstacles. As Sun Zi says in *The Art of War*, "If you know your enemy and know yourself, you need not fear the results of a hundred battles."

Overreacting to our personal past is the first barrier we must seek to conquer. The following steps can help you evaluate the areas where you may be overreacting because of your personal past.

1. Describe your and your spouse's childhood experiences. Take time to think about it, and discuss it with one another or a trusted friend.

2. Take out a piece of paper and list what your parents (or primary caregivers) did well and what they did poorly.

3. Make another list of your positive and negative childhood experiences. Next to the positive and negative experiences, rate them on a scale of 1–10, one being the worst and ten being the best.

4. Write what effect your positive and negative childhood experience had or still has on you for better or worse. This may take some hard self-reflection and perhaps even external input from someone who knows you well. See Appendix A for a chart to help you with this exercise.

By beginning with your parents' best practices and your most positive learning experiences, you will create a foundation for your own parenting philosophy. This exercise alone can be very revealing as you evaluate your own child-training practices.

Think about the effect your childhood has on your parenting. For example, adults who grew up in families where they had to work without much playtime may overcompensate by creating constant entertainment for their children. Adults who grew up poor may lavish gifts on their children without teaching them the importance of savings or frugality. Parents who were never told the reason behind commands may explain everything to their child before expecting obedience (and receive little). All of these imbalances have natural historical sources. However, overcompensating could hurt your children in their development toward maturity. It is crucial for parents to think honestly about their own upbringing to determine the degree to which it is influencing their parenting decisions. The important thing is to identify those experiences and effects and to choose to build parenting practices around them that produce the best results. We have a choice: either to recover from our past or to repeat it again with our children.

The second barrier to overcome is a combination of fear and defensiveness. Most of us have learned to receive constructive criticism in the arenas of education, work, hobbies, and sports. But when others suggest that our children are flawed or that we may be falling short in our parenting, most of us become highly defensive. Hidden fears and insecurities can keep us from looking honestly at our current parenting practices. These fears need to be overcome because our children's emotional, spiritual, social, and professional future is at stake. Most people seek very little parent training other than what was modeled in their own homes growing up. Parents need to be active learners regarding current dangers in our child's world. Today's environment presents different challenges and threats that did not exist for our parents' generation. If your child is your most valuable treasure, you should seek more training in parenting than in any other area of your life.

We all need to be open to improving our parenting techniques. If we become defensive and refuse to look critically at our current patterns, then we are like a stubborn person who will not go to the hospital for fear he may hear bad news. Don't limp along with sick or weak parenting techniques. Be a learner and improve every day in this critical area of parenting. Change is hard and painful at times. But when the pain and embarrassment of a child's misbehavior outweighs the pain of change, you will change. Personally, I would rather go through the pain of training than the pain of regret.

Underestimating humanity's fallenness is the third barrier. The thought of human nature being basically good is a nice idea, but it has very little proof. Children do not have to be taught to do wrong and disobey. They need to be taught to do right. A wise leader named Solomon once said in Proverbs 22:15, "Foolishness is bound up in the heart of a child" (NASB).

The Minnesota Crime Commission issued a report in 1926 summing up the human condition in the following quote:

> Every baby starts life as a little savage. He is completely selfish and self-centered. He wants what he wants when he wants it: his bottle, his mother's attention, his playmate's toys, his uncle's watch, or whatever. Deny him these and he seethes with rage and aggressiveness, which would be murderous were he not so helpless. He's dirty; he has no morals, no knowledge, and no developed skills. This means that all children are born delinquent. If permitted to continue in their self-centered world of infancy, given free reign to their impulsive actions to satisfy every want, every child would grow up a criminal, a thief, a killer, a rapist.[2]

In my own experience, training little savages to become knights and princesses of virtue requires hard work, perseverance, and planning—not to mention a lot of praying for wisdom when I don't know what to do.

The fourth and final barrier is the mistake of overdelegating. Overdelegating is a symptom of our modern industrial society. Parents experience an overwhelming feeling of responsibility, combined with ill-preparedness, when they bring their first child home from the hospital and typically face this daunting job with no formal training. As our children grow, we hope we are doing a good job, but our minds are often filled with doubts. Our fears and doubts are confirmed when our children misbehave or embarrass us by throwing a fit in public. This is where we make a conscious decision to outsource the training of our children to the so-called experts.

Many societies believe that children can be best trained in state institutions (public school, kindergarten, child care, etc.). These institutions do play important roles in training our children, but training in morals and character has to happen in the home. Some teachers or experts may have life philosophies that would not pass your approval. Even if our children learn to behave at school, once they return home they will resume old habits of behavior. I have heard parents say with bewilderment, "I don't understand it. My child behaves at school, but they will not obey at home." The truth is that they have not been trained to behave at home. What long-term effect will such a dichotomized world have on a child's future? Many children have learned to behave in kindergarten and school, but when it comes to family and social interaction outside of structured institutions, they are undisciplined and totally selfish. If we fail to train our children at home, we will produce untrained, dysfunctional adults in marriage, friendships, and extended-family relationships. In short, the child who has not trained at home as well as at school could have a very difficult adult life. You need to train your child to behave at home: your child's future and happiness depends on it.

As parents, we can easily lose sight of how we are doing. Growing up on one of the Great Lakes of Michigan was a lot of fun as a kid. On hot summer days we would enjoy sitting on inner tubes, floating out in the water. With the sun beating down and the soft lapping of the water, it was nice to just close our eyes and float. The problem came when we relaxed too long without paying attention to the wind and the direction we were floating. It was possible to drift out a couple hundred yards from the shore in a very short time. With great effort, we could either paddle back or wait for someone to come out with a boat and rescue us. In the same way, it is easy for the winds of culture to cause you and your children to drift far off course. As parents, we need to have clear goals and attentive eyes in order to keep our children on course. Keeping the end goal in mind will be crucial in raising exceptional children.

While running the marathon at the 1968 Summer Olympics in Mexico City, John Stephen Akhwari of Tanzania cramped up due to the high altitude of the city. He had not trained at such an altitude back in his country. At the nineteen-kilometer point during the forty-two-kilometer race, some runners jockeyed for position, and Akhwari was hit. He fell, badly dislocating his knee and hitting his shoulder hard against the pavement. However, he continued running, finishing last among the fifty-seven competitors who completed the race (seventy-five had started). The winner of the marathon, Mamo Wolde of Ethiopia, finished in two hours, twenty minutes, and twenty-six seconds. Akhwari finished in three hours, twenty-five minutes, and twenty-seven seconds, when the sun had set and there were only a few thousand people left in the stadium. A television crew was sent from the medal ceremony when word arrived that one more runner was about to finish. As Akhwari finally crossed the finish line, a cheer came from the small crowd. When interviewed later and asked why he continued running, Akhwari said, "My country did not send me five thousand miles to start the race. They sent me five thousand miles to finish the race."[3]

You may feel like that injured runner sometimes, barely hobbling along, but remember that your children need you not just to start, but to finish. They need you to overcome your negative family patterns and to gain victory over your personal fear and defensiveness in order to deal with their need for training. But, most of all, they need you to be their parents and not delegate that responsibility to others. Our kids need us, and we, with God's help, can be great loving parents.

Application points:
- What did you learn from this chapter that you would like to implement?
- Which of the following barriers do you need to work on overcoming: overcompensating, being fearful, being overly defensive, underestimating human depravity, or overdelegating?
- Who could help encourage you to overcome these barriers?
- How would you like to start?

Chapter 15

· ·

Creating a Family Vision

· ·

As selfishness and complaint pervert the mind,
so love with its joy clears and sharpens the vision.

—Helen Keller

Love should be the motivating factor in establishing a united family vision. Without a vision or plan for success, a family will suffer and take on the shape of its cultural surroundings. A vision for a family is something that both parents need to embrace. My wife Carolyn and I come from very different family backgrounds. Her parents divorced when she was just four years old. Both parents remarried, and she grew up spending time in both homes. Her parents tried all they could to minimize the negative effects of divorce, but the hurt and challenges were unavoidable. I, on the other hand, grew up with parents who loved each other deeply. I never doubted their love for each other, and as a result, my childhood was filled with many happy memories.

My wonderful childhood was interrupted, however, when my mother had an unwelcome onset of cancer. She was diagnosed with breast cancer when I was in junior high. We still had five good years as a family until she passed away and went to be with God. I was twenty-one at that time. It was a trying time for our whole family. My oldest brother was married, but my younger sister had just graduated from high school and my youngest brother was still in high school. Our family went from happy and functional to somewhat dysfunctional. Each member, dealing with grief and loss in their own way, caused some miscommunication and conflict.

I am sure you and your spouse will also have differences in your family backgrounds. These differences can become strengths if you can develop a united family vision from them. The following four activities will help you begin developing a united family vision.

1. Describe what a good family looks like. Talk about it as a family, or write it out separately and then compare what you have written.

2. Discuss what is required to maintain your description of a good family (internal and external factors, family rules, external activities, clubs, social groups, or church youth groups, etc.).

3. Develop a family mission statement.

4. Create a SMART goal to help you get started. (Appendix B will help you with the above activities.)

Your family mission statement will articulate your values and will remind you of your goal. It can help create daily habits in your home that will become the foundation of your family. Family mentors can encourage and model a picture of success. I find in my own family, I am continually evaluating our daily habits in light of what I want our children to remember after they leave our home. I want to establish strong family habits in order to model values that our children can repeat in their own families. We developed together our family mission statement, which is as follows:

Foster Family Mission Statement
Love God and love each other.
Live to be a blessing.
Let God's word, Christ's example, and the Holy Spirit be our guide.

Family verse:
"I was young and now I am old, yet I have never seen the
righteous forsaken or their children begging bread. They are
always generous and lend freely; their children will be blessed."
—Psalm 37:25-26

As a parent, what is your hope for your children? Most parents want more for their children than to just contribute to society and make enough money to provide for their family. We want to see our children excel in their gifting and reach their full potential. We want to raise our children to mature so as to be role models and leaders for others to follow. In short, we want them to step into the roles that knights and princesses fulfilled during the Dark Ages in Europe. This is a rather lofty goal that will require our children to be trained in maturity to reach their personal best.

If this is one of our goals, we need to answer the question, "What is maturity?" For my children, this involves three virtues: self-control, wisdom, and responsibility.

Self-control means they have control over their emotions, passions, desires, and temper. They are able to do what they ought to do even when their emotions are telling them otherwise. It involves the ability to act selflessly by showing kindness to others, to consider others' needs as more important than their own, and to show deference. This is a very high, but attainable goal. I do not expect a two-year-old or even an eight-year-old to always get it right. And I will consider my child still in training until these virtues are consistently practiced in their lives.

The next virtue to develop in our children is wisdom. A great deal of wisdom is learned as one gets older and experiences more of life's challenges and joys. However, our children need to learn the foundations of wisdom and how to grow in it. They need to be taught how to learn from personal experience and by watching others. I had many discussions with my daughter about the decisions she and her friends were making. Some of her friends were making wise decisions worthy of praise and emulation. Other friends were making unwise decisions useful as warnings. Through these discussions, I taught her how to learn from the successes and failures of others. Such coaching can save our children from having to experience many hard mistakes and yet still be wise in those areas. They also need to learn how to make good decisions in the midst of a multitude of choices. That is why it is important for us to let our children make choices appropriate to their maturity level as they grow so they will learn the art of decision-making.

Learning to become responsible is the last basic virtue of maturity. We must teach our children that their actions have consequences. They are responsible for their own actions, and they will reap the benefit or the negative consequence of their choices. This involves good work habits as well as faithfulness to follow through on commitments. These three basic virtues of self-control, wisdom, and responsibility will create a wonderful foundation for your child's success.

Having described what maturity looks like, let me take a minute and describe immaturity. A child who is not taught to control their emotions, passions, desires, and temper when they are young will face many difficulties as an adult. During the teen years, self-indulgent children will increasingly demand more rights and privileges (Internet time, music preferences, time with friends, time on the phone, etc.), even though they may not have proven themselves as responsible. They seldom see the relationship between being responsible and receiving privileges. I at times reminded my children that they had very few rights and mostly privileges. Privileges are given only when maturity and gratefulness are present.

I sat down with a friend at lunch just the other day and listened to him as he expressed his concern for his daughter who was listening to music he was not pleased with. She was also, in his opinion, spending too much time online chatting with other kids that he didn't know. I encouraged him to remind his daughter that these activities (time listening to music, Internet time) were privileges and not rights. The continuation of such privileges depended on her appropriate actions and attitude. I have no doubt that a challenge was sure to come from his daughter, but with a united parental front, my friend could continue to lovingly train his princess toward maturity.

When a self-indulgent child becomes an adult, they are characterized most often as selfish and unhappy. Self-indulgent children were taught or led to believe that the world exists to make them happy. In their adult life, the world will not seek to make them happy and will most likely consistently let them down. Self-indulgent adults and children are often angry because they don't get what they want. They feel cheated, and since they have not learned to control their own emotions, others are less likely to enjoy being around them. This means they will have fewer friends than their peers.

Sad to say, most children today could be characterized as self-indulgent. This doesn't need to be the case for your child in your home. Loving parents can identify areas of immaturity in their children and train them toward maturity. There will be an especially hard road ahead for parents with older children accustomed to getting their own way. However, the saying "better late than never" definitely applies to parents and children in this situation. The future happiness of your knight or princess depends on you training them to maturity. And that means training them to know that they are not the center of the universe. They need to learn to control their own emotions in order to grow into mature adults.

When planning for the future, fearful parents see the challenges and become paralyzed. They create no plan for the future. Timid parents let the popular culture lead their family. Following the popular culture hasn't proven to be successful for the human race. Good parents see the challenges and proactively create a plan and vision that makes what seems impossible to become possible. They literally make the future into a better place one child at a time.

> *The positive thinker sees the invisible, feels the intangible,*
> *and achieves the impossible.*
> —Winston Churchill

You can train your child to maturity. It is not impossible. It can be done, and you can do it.

Application points:
- What did you learn from this chapter that you would like to implement?
- Which of the basic virtues for maturity would you like to focus on first: self-control, wisdom, or responsibility?
- When would you like to begin creating a family mission statement?

Chapter 16

. . . .

Child Training in the Home

. . . .

There's no place like home,
There's no place like home,
There's no place like home.

—Dorothy, *Wizard of Oz*

Most of the qualities that create success or failure in a child will come from lessons learned at home. School will play a significant role in expanding your child's knowledge and in equipping them with knowledge for a career. These things are important, but character, moral behavior, and self-esteem are all nurtured in the context of a loving home.

Parents naturally place a great deal of focused attention on their child's education and the environment in which they learn. Education is the process by which a child learns knowledge that is not self-evident. Such information comes from the outside and is assimilated into the child's understanding. Training, on the other hand, is the process by which a child learns to control personal desires, behaviors, and emotions. It can be said that teaching is primarily a mental mind exercise while training is learning the exercise of controlling and mastering the will, and thus the ability to control one's behavior.

Just as a child is taught the sound and meaning of new words, they are trained how to live out the meaning of those words in socially acceptable ways and at appropriate volumes, depending on the circumstances. Child training begins much earlier than teaching. Children are trained in regards to eating and sleeping just after birth. Some children during the first weeks of life are trained to eat at certain times, while others are trained to eat whenever they express they are hungry. A child can be trained to go to sleep in total quietness or with soft music playing or in the middle of a noisy home. They are also trained to sleep in the arms of a loved one or in a cradle or crib. Everything from sleeping, walking, talking, and playing are all within the realm of child training.

A common mistake is to assume that once someone is taught a behavior, they have been trained. For example: If an employer trains his workers to perform a certain job, but after the training is finished they still cannot do the job satisfactorily, then they have not been effectively trained. They were instructed, but learning or mastery of the skill did not occur. In the same way, a child cannot be counted as "trained" until they behave in the manner honoring and acceptable to their parents.

Earlier this year, our youngest son Adam had a moment when he became very upset while at our friend's home because he didn't get his way. He grew silent and looked like he was about to cry. Out of embarrassment, he quickly left the room and went upstairs to the bedroom. Our host saw his struggle and was very concerned about him. I simply said he was still in training, and I went up and talked with him until the issue was resolved. After a few minutes, he rejoined us and entered into the evening activities even though they were not his favorite activities. It was a wonderful "knight in training" moment with my son. It is important that we do not give up on training our knights and princesses until their behavior blesses others and honors their parents.

I like the meaning of the Hebrew word associated with training children, which is *gadal*, or "to rear" in English. It literally means to "twist unto greatness." The Hebrew concept involves twisting children from their selfish nature into greatness. Twisting a child's nature is sure to come with resistance and will call for perseverance and commitment in order to reach the goal. There is another Hebrew word that has a profound meaning when it comes to parenting. The word is *shema*. This word means "to listen" or "to hear." The Shema is also a creed found in the book of Deuteronomy in the Bible. It teaches about our relationship with God and how we can transmit our values to our children. It says:

> *Love the LORD your God with all your heart and with all*
> *your soul and with all your strength. These commandments*
> *that I give you today are to be upon your hearts. Impress them*
> *on your children. Talk about them when you sit at home and*
> *when you walk along the road, when you lie down and when*

you get up. Tie them as symbols on your hands and bind
them on your foreheads. Write them on the doorframes of
your houses and on your gates.
—Deuteronomy 6:5–9

Within the Shema are keys to instilling our values in our children. We can seek ways to talk to our children at home, on the way to school, at the grocery store, etc., about what they should believe and think. Kids today already have their values written on their t-shirts; they have them in their hands via text messages from friends; they place posters on their walls and over their doors. Values are being reinforced on a continual basis. As parents, we need to be actively involved in choosing proper values for our children. Values will be embraced when parents model and talk about what they believe in a natural setting in and around the home.

I conducted a research study in China regarding values and role models, with more than five hundred students filling out questionnaires. The study supported that children most often select their parents as role models. It is true that some, for short periods of time, will look up to famous musicians or world-class athletes. However, at the end of the day, kids want to brag to their friends about their parents.

The Bible says that parents are the pride of their children. This is good news for all of us parents. Our kids are looking for reasons to be proud of us, which is both encouraging and challenging at the same time. This is encouraging because we don't have to worry about getting their attention. This is challenging in that we need to spend time with them so that they can see what makes us tick. You don't have to be a superstar to impress your child. If you have a cool job (which most of us don't), they can use that to be proud of you, or they will brag about the time you spend with them. For example, your knight or princess may say: my dad takes me out for dates, fishing, road trips, to McDonald's, shooting basketball, playing video games, etc. Any reason we give them for such pride, our kids will take it and use it. Other kids may have world-renowned parents, but the parent your child will learn the most from is you. No superstar or superathlete will ever take your place as life-long trainer and role model. Our children will go through phases where they hang a poster of someone they admire in their room. However, when they don't know how to act or what to think in a given situation, they will model what they learned at home by watching you (scary, I know).

No matter what background you came from, you should strive to be the best parent you can be. Whether your child is ten months, ten years, or fifty years old, you're still their parents. Your role in their life will vary greatly through the years, but you will always be their parent and it is never too late to try to correct mistakes you've made in the past. For some, you may even have a second chance to parent as you spend time with your grandchildren. Whether you are father, mother, grandmother, or grandfather, you all play a vital role in training those children under your care. Embrace your role and commit to doing it to the best of your ability. Remember, the next generation is watching and learning from you. The following poem is a good reminder for all parents:

"When You Thought I Wasn't Looking"
by Mary Rita Schilke Sill[1]
Written for my mother, Blanche Schilke.

When you thought I wasn't looking
You hung my first painting on the refrigerator
And I wanted to paint another.

When you thought I wasn't looking
You fed a stray cat
And I thought it was good to be kind to animals.

When you thought I wasn't looking
You baked a birthday cake just for me
And I knew that little things were special things.

When you thought I wasn't looking
You said a prayer
And I believed there was a God I could always talk to.

When you thought I wasn't looking
You kissed me good-night
And I felt loved.

When you thought I wasn't looking
I saw tears come from your eyes
And I learned that sometimes things hurt –
But that it's alright to cry.

When you thought I wasn't looking
You smiled
And it made me want to look that pretty too.

When you thought I wasn't looking
You cared
And I wanted to be everything I could be.

When you thought I wasn't looking
I looked …
And wanted to say thanks
For all the things you did
When you thought I wasn't looking.

Application points:
- What did you learn from this chapter that you would like to implement?
- How can you create more time for training in your home?
- In what ways can you be a role model for your child?
- How can your child see you in action?

Chapter 17

Training Through Role-Play
(Good, Better, Best)

*My son, do not make light of the Lord's discipline,
and do not lose heart when he rebukes you,
because the Lord disciplines those He loves.*

—Hebrews 12:5–6

Discipline your son, for in that there is hope.

—Proverbs 19:18

A close friend of mine was called for jury duty. During the interview process to select jurors for the trial, one of the lawyers asked him what was more important for parenting—love or obedience and respect. He thought about it and said he believed the two could not be separated, reasoning that if you love your child, you will teach them to respect and obey you. This answer upset the lawyer, who argued that love was most important. In the end, my friend was excused from jury duty, which allowed him to return home. A home filled with his loving wife (soon to give birth to a baby girl) and two energetic loving, respectful, obedient boys. Your children need to know that you love them and because of your love you discipline and correct them.

As parents, our days are full of many activities and interruptions, and many of those interruptions from our children are actually valuable training opportunities. Busyness can cause us to miss out on ideal chances for training our children to become knights and princesses. In this chapter, we will be looking at ways to schedule time for training your young knights and princesses, just as you schedule other activities during the day. A little training on the positive side can go a long way in reducing the time spent on disciplining negative behavior.

When our children were young, we would sometimes role-play good and bad behavior. I would knock at the door and pretend to be a guest coming over for the evening. The children would decide on a behavior style. They had the most fun pretending to be rude or silly. We would let them role model the bad behavior just for fun. Then we would instruct them in how to practice different appropriate greetings. For example, if I would say hello and ask them their name, they would return the greeting and give their name. We considered acceptable behavior to be responding respectfully and loudly enough to be clearly understood when an adult asked them a question. If they responded with good eye contact in a clear voice and extended their hand for a handshake, we let them know this was even better behavior. Best behavior had to go one step further, such as showing interest in the guest by inquiring how their trip went, or asking them if they would like something to drink, or helping them with their coat. We taught them this was the best behavior. Naturally, we needed to tell them about the different types of behavior, but letting them practice it as a role-play was a fun way for them to learn the different ways to respond, and we encouraged them to strive for their best behavior.

Correcting our children's bad behavior is an important part of good parenting. As part of effective parenting, it is crucial that we make it clear to them the type of behavior we expect. Training them in advance in the appropriate behavior can save a lot of frustration for parents and children. Role-play training can be very effective in setting standards for behavior inside the home as well as outside of the home. For example, the grocery store or market can be a trying experience when young children see a favorite fruit, candy, or shiny toy. They can be relentless in their pleading for the item. Administering correction in any form in such a public place is not very convenient. A proactive approach to prevent such embarrassing moments is to train children at home before they are in the situation. Let them know they are going to see things while shopping that they will want. Be clear as to what they are to do. Some parents tell their children in advance they will get one treat (a piece of fruit, a sweet, a small item, or a toy) on the trip to the store. Other times, they may be told in advance that they can go but will not be getting anything on that day. Both situations can be practiced at home. Appropriate behavior on such outings can be rewarded by verbal praise or treats once they return home.

The best time to begin training children is while they are still toddlers. Setting aside as little as five to fifteen minutes per day to train your child in appropriate responses can make a big difference. Such training can begin at a very early age. For example, while your child is sitting on the other side of the room, in a normal voice, call them to come to you. If they come to you, praise them and repeat the process. If they don't, go over to them, look them in the eye and tell them they need to obey when you tell them to do something, and administer appropriate discipline. Return to the other side of the room and tell them to come to you again. Praise them if they obey. Discipline them if they do not. Once they consistently obey, repeat the process a few times in order to reinforce the concept.[1] If you have time that day or the next, you can practice calling them from a different room. Your child will likely enjoy this training time and think of it as a game. In most cases, it will only take minutes for your children to learn to obey during training time. They will likely look forward to the times you do this with them in your home. Once children are trained in the home, enforcing the same obedience outside the home is much easier and is a natural progression in training.

As children learn to talk, it is important to train them in respectful ways to respond when told to do something. We required our kids to verbally respond to us when we asked them to do something with a simple, "Yes, Mom" or "Yes, Dad." This helped us know they heard us and affirmed they were making the correct choice to obey.

Children also need to be trained in how to ask for what they want. It still baffles me how children can make themselves seem twice their weight by wiggling and squirming! Hold a child on your hip or arm, and you will know when they want to get down by their sudden "weight gain." Teaching them to say "May I please get down" is a simple thing for them to learn. If children are let down when they squirm or fuss, they will continue to do that each time they want to get down. However, the next time they start squirming or fussing to get down, hold them tight and instruct them to ask politely, "May I please get down?" As soon as they reply appropriately, set them down. Simple behavior like this can also be practiced at home during training times. Other settings for training can include:

- Greeting friends
- Playing in the park
- Helping elderly people
- Traveling on a bus or in a car

By role-playing these events in advance, you can create patterns of acceptable behavior in your child's mind. When they have the opportunity to perform in real life what they have practiced in the home, they will do it with excitement. They may even look for opportunities to show what they have learned in practice. Role-plays can keep training on a positive note. Rather than constantly telling children what they have done wrong, training in the home gives opportunities for praise. Praising children for doing what they have learned is a great joy of many parents. When role-played behavior becomes instinctive behavior for your children, you will know they have been trained. Taking the time is the key to success, and those who take the time to instruct their children at home will enjoy the benefit for years to come.

> *"The family should be a closely knit group. The home should be a self-contained shelter of security; a kind of school where life's basic lessons are taught; and a kind of church where God is honored; a place where wholesome recreation and simple pleasures are enjoyed."*
> —Billy Graham

Application points:
- What did you learn from this chapter that you would like to implement?
- What behaviors would you like to train your child through role-play?
- When can you schedule your first role-play training time?

Chapter 18

· · · · · · · · · ·

Intimidated Parents
and Child-Run Homes

· · · · · · · · · ·

*The thing that impresses me most about America
is the way parents obey their children.*

—Edward, Duke of Windsor[1]

Parenting is such a daunting task, with an incredible amount of internal and external pressure to do it "right"; it is no wonder that many parents feel intimidated. Today many parents are struggling with keeping their child under control. It's not that they don't love their child and want them to obey; it's just that they don't know what a controlled child looks like. A controlled child is one who obeys their parent's request the first time they are told to do something. They do so without complaining or arguing. They speak to their parent in a respectful voice even when they do not get what they desire or understand the request. Does this sound too good to be true?

Gaining control of our children is the first part in having a parent-run home. Just the thought of having to gain control of a home may sound strange, but the reality is that many homes today are child-run. Children have intimidated their parents into letting them be in charge. Intimidated parents have all but given up on the hope of training their child. They look forward to the day when their child's behavioral training can be someone else's responsibility. What are some signs of an intimidated parent?

An intimidated parent:

1. Seeks to explain to their child the rightness of their decisions in order to convince their child to obey.

2. Fears making their child mad at them.

3. Becomes emotionally weakened when they fail to gain their child's approval.

4. Lets their child argue back and enters into the argument.

5. Attempts to regain the child's approval by offering privileges or candy after administering discipline.

6. Hurts deeply if their young child in anger says, "I hate you."[2]

Parenting can be a great joy, but if you have become an intimidated parent, that joy has been taken from you. Intimidated parents will lose control of the home and ultimately the respect of their child. Losing control of the home will result in a child-run home. In a child-run home, all decisions are made or influenced by the child. No parent says in their heart, "I am going to give the authority of our home over to my child and let them run things their way." Child-run homes develop from lack of proper training or by giving in to our children little by little. In a child-run home, parents will often say things like:

- "I prepare two meals every night, one for the adults and one for our child."

- "When we go out to eat, we can only go to a few restaurants because little _____ doesn't enjoy any others."

- "We could never go to that activity because our child would be bored and would misbehave."

- "We are going to change schools because our child doesn't like the teachers at his school."[3]

Parents who say their child just "refuses to do something or won't behave unless certain favorable conditions are met" have lost control and need to take steps to regain control of their home. They have given their child veto power over decisions. Such power will not produce a happy, satisfied child. Rather, a child with too much control in the home will be stressed and irritable. The child has been put in a place of leadership by their parents, when inwardly they want to be led. Children in a child-run home will get away with interrupting, whining, manipulating, and interrupting adults while they are talking. They will demand that their needs are more important than the parents'. At this point, you could be coming to the conclusion that it takes a lot of work to keep a home from becoming a child-run home. But be encouraged by the following advice: "Discipline your son, and he will give you peace; he will bring delight to your soul" (Proverbs 29:17).

A home doesn't become a child-run home when parents make occasional lapses in child-training. It happens when children are consistently allowed to continue in the above-mentioned behaviors. To encourage you, let me give some examples of what is possible when children are properly trained in respectful behavior. In this home a child will not interrupt parents when they are talking to other adults unless it is an emergency. They will obey parents the first time they are asked to do something. Children will serve others and in so doing learn how much joy can be found in serving. They will also speak to parents in a tone of voice that honors them. This type of home is a joy to live in. It is also a wonderful environment for entertaining extended family and friends. The opposite is true of a home where the child is the one in control.

You may be wondering why parents share authority with their children. Here are four common reasons among many: First, some parents think it is politically correct to exercise democracy in the home. They may feel that everyone in the home should have an equal say in what happens. This is hard for children because when Mom and Dad are in disagreement, the child's vote makes the final decision. This causes the child stress because they must choose one parent over the other. Children do need to learn responsibility, but part of growing into maturity is learning how to submit to the decisions of others. When your child reaches adulthood, they will not be asked their opinions on everything that affects them at work or in their personal life. To give them such an expectation from childhood sets them up for major disappointments as adults.

A child-run home can also result from lack of unity between parents or grandparents sharing the parenting duties. If the adults caring for the child cannot agree on consistent parenting practices, the child will be confused at best. Most likely they will feel insecure and anxious, not knowing what behavior will be accepted. Even if the child learns the different standards for each caregiver, they are still in danger of getting caught in the middle of disagreements. It is so much better when the adults can agree on parenting methods.

The most common underlying cause of a child-run home is insecurity. The parents often lack the confidence to lead their child. They fear rejection and seek the approval from their child in their parenting methods. This situation is a disaster for the insecure parent for the following reason: parents of child-run homes become disrespected by their children, and in the end the child also feels cheated. It's natural for parents to want their children to love and appreciate them. This can happen with strong, loving discipline. I will talk more about how to win your child's respect in the next chapter.

I would like to close with a poem about a little lamb. We may be timid and possibly even intimidated at times, but let's remember that God can give us strength to care for His precious little lambs that He has given us to raise.

"The Lamb"
by William Blake (1757–1827)

Little Lamb, who made thee?
Dost thou know who made thee?
Gave thee life & bid thee feed,
By the stream & o'ver the mead;
Gave thee clothing of delight,
Softest clothing, wooly, bright;
Gave thee such a tender voice,
Making all the vales rejoice?
Little Lamb, who made thee?
Dost thou know who made thee?

Little Lamb, I'll tell thee,
Little Lamb, I'll tell thee:
He is called by thy name,
For He calls himself a Lamb.
He is meek & He is mild;
He became a little child.
I a child & Thou a lamb.
We are called by His name.
Little Lamb, God bless thee!
Little Lamb, God bless thee!

Application points:

- What did you learn from this chapter that you would like to implement?
- In what areas does your home characterize a child-run home?
- What do you need to change personally to maintain or regain authority in your home?

Chapter 19

Regaining Authority

Tis a lesson you should heed, Try, try again;
If at first you don't succeed, Try, try again;
Then your courage should appear,
For, if you will persevere,
You will conquer, never fear; Try, try again.

—Palmer's Teacher's Manual[1]

Regaining authority in the home is best accomplished with a united mission by both parents. It will be one of those endeavors that will require perseverance, consistency, and trying and trying again. Whether you are establishing or reclaiming authority in the home, your success is crucial to the future success and happiness of your child. A loving home that has the proper authority structure will be a well-ordered home. A child trained in submitting to parental authority in the home will:

- obey parents the first time they are asked to do something.
- obey without whining or complaining.
- obey household rules even when they are not being watched.

A controlled child learns to obey parents out of respect even when they don't understand or agree with what they are being asked to do. There are times when children can appeal a parent's decision, and this is discussed more fully in Chapter 22. First, they must learn to trust their parents' authority and respect their decisions. Establishing parental authority in the home is beneficial to your child for the following reasons:

- When a child learns to control their outward behavior by obeying, they also gain inner control.

- When a child is allowed to have authority in the home and challenge parental decisions, they take on responsibility for running the home. This responsibility will be resented even though they fight for it because they are not emotionally mature enough to handle it. Stress and insecurity will be the result.

- A child is more likely to have trouble obeying authority figures outside the home if they are used to arguing and getting their own way at home.

- Quick obedience to parental commands can save a child's life when it is threatened by a moving car, fast bicycle, electrical wires, or other hazards.

- A child with well-defined borders for behavior can relax. They learn that by remaining within established boundaries, they are safe. A child also feels more secure when they have solid, consistent behavioral expectations.

Parent-run homes are a safe place for play and imagination when the child is trained in obedience. I once heard of a school that experimented with freedom from rules and boundaries. They had a fenced-in area for the children to play during recess. When they took the fence down, they expected the children to roam about more freely. But the opposite happened. Instead of exploring the area beyond where the fence used to be, the children grouped more closely to the center of the play area. In the past, they would play right up to the fence in all areas of the playground. The fenceless playground no longer had set boundaries, and as a result, the children created for themselves a smaller area for play to make up for the lack of structure. This example reinforces the fact that children thrive in well-structured environments in which to explore and create. They don't need stifling boundaries, but if you provide no boundaries at all, they will seek to create their own.

Some parents may argue that their child is just strong-willed and refuses to be trained in obedience. Others may have experienced that disciplining their child has just served to increase their bad behavior and disobedience. The strong-willed child may be harder to train in obedience than a docile child, but they need (and desire) training all the more.

If discipline is not administered correctly, it is possible for discipline to actually strengthen the will of the child rather than bring it into submission.

This happens when parents attempt to exercise authority in the home, but stop short of accomplishing it. They discipline, but not to the point of bringing about repentance and humility. They seek to take control of a decision, but in the end let the child decide. A child needs to learn that they are not the final authority. This means they have to lose arguments waged against their parent. They need to obey the parent's decisions even when they don't like them. When this happens, the child learns they are no longer in control and soon will rest in the fact that they are just children and that Mom and Dad are back in charge.

Regaining authority in the home also involves regaining your child's respect. If your home is child-run, you have already lost your child's respect. Obeying those we do not respect is difficult for adults as well as children. So how do we go about regaining our child's respect? What must parents do?

The first step in gaining a child's respect is to train your child to obey your word. A parent should speak a command once in a normal, calm, clear tone, and the child should obey what is asked. The parent who raises their voice, threatens, but in the end never follows through on their threats will not be respected. They will only be looked at with contempt. When your child disobeys a command, a negative consequence must consistently be given.

Second, authority once taken back must not be returned to the child. This does not mean that you never ask your child what they want or would like to do. It does mean that when you make the final decision, you do not allow your child to manipulate you into changing your mind so that they can get what they want. Once authority is regained, it must not be given back. Parents who sporadically try to take authority back, but through neglect or exhaustion give in to their child, will not be respected. The child will gain little from this and will resent the parent for their inconsistency.

Third, do not allow your child to talk to you with disrespect. A child, when given opportunity, will talk to their parents in the same way they would talk to a peer. A child can be taught to speak to adults with greater respect. They can be taught that it is disrespectful to talk back to or argue with adults. All of our children talked to us disrespectfully at one point in their upbringing.

The first time it happened, we simply instructed them that such a tone or comment was not appropriate. They were not rebellious, they were just learning. If they continued with disrespectful tones or comments once instructed, then we disciplined them for inappropriate behavior.

Fourth, when teaching your child respect, don't expect their approval, support, or affection. Affection from a child will come and go as they learn to control their emotions. When a child realizes that their parent's emotions are dependent on their constant affection, they will be tempted to manipulate. They could say things like, "I hate you," "I will never talk to you again," or "I don't love you." The secure parent can accept these manipulative statements for what they are (manipulation and immaturity). A parent who needs to know their child consistently loves them will be handicapped in training them in self-control. Insecure parents are not able to discipline appropriately for fear they will lose their child's love and approval.[2] The child loses out since the parent is not able to exercise strong leadership. Parents need to remember that they are the parents and the children need to learn maturity from them. Moms and dads are the primary source for learning lessons needed for a successful life. Listen to what one famous leader said about his mother.

> *My mother was the most beautiful woman I ever saw. All that I am I owe to my mother, I attribute all my success in life to the moral, intellectual, and physical education I received from her.*
> —George Washington[3]

Application points:
- What did you learn from this chapter that you would like to implement?
- In what areas do you need to regain authority in your home?
- Who can help and support you as you train your child in obedience and respect?
- What will your first step be?

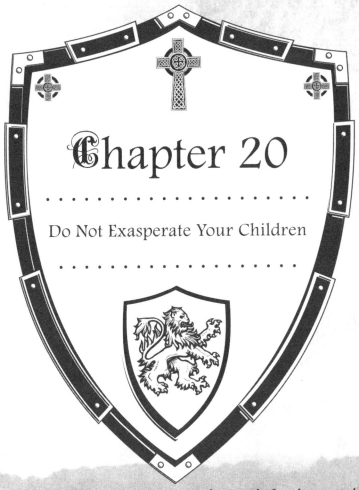

Chapter 20

Do Not Exasperate Your Children

Children, obey your parents in the Lord, for this is right. "Honor your father and mother"—which is the first commandment with a promise—"that it may go well with you and that you may enjoy long life on the earth." Fathers, do not exasperate your children; instead, bring them up in the training and instruction of the Lord.

—Ephesians 6:1–4

I attended a teaching seminar where the opening speaker gave statistics on how bad the behavior of students had become. The common agreement among most teachers was that it's the parents' fault that children are so poorly disciplined today. The speaker's reply was interesting. He said, "Parents aren't keeping the good, well-behaved kids at home; the kids they send you are the best kids they have." So, in short, he was saying, "Stop using your energy to complain and get to work helping the children become better people." Teachers can do their part, but character needs to be taught at home. No parent wants their child to disrespect them or other adults. No parent wants his or her child to whine, manipulate, and disobey. We all want our children to be model citizens who honor us while being a blessing to the community. So what can we as parents do that we are not already doing?

Most chapters in this book focus on what parents can do; however, this chapter will focus on what parents need to stop doing. There are many behaviors that will undermine our ability to train our children. These behaviors will actually exasperate our children[1] and undermine any of the good parenting practices we implement. Take gardening for example: We can plant the best seeds in the richest soil. We can provide the right amount of water and fertilizer. However, if we do not remove the weeds from the garden and protect the plants from harsh conditions, they will not grow to bear good fruit. Let me list some weeds and harsh conditions that will provoke your child to anger and undermine your best attempts at effectively training your child.

First, lack of unity in marriage is a common problem that happens in a lot of homes. "For this reason a man will leave his father and mother and be united to his wife, and they will become one flesh" (Genesis 2:24). The best gift you can give your children is a strong, loving relationship with your spouse. This is a hard one to start with because it takes both parents to accomplish a strong marriage, and it is likely that only one of you is reading this book. You might be in a place to share this with your spouse, but better still, make the changes you can make to improve your marriage. This is the best way you can love your child today.

Second, not taking time "just to talk" will hinder your relationship with your child. "Communication is the foundation of relationship," and the same is true of a relationship with your child. As they grow, they will learn how to communicate from you. As you listen to them, they will learn to listen to others. As they learn to share their feelings, fears, and disappointments with you, your relationship will grow as they grow. I remember our daughter sharing that she was shocked to find out that some of her teenage friends didn't talk to their parents about what was bothering them. She said, "I talk to you about everything." I went to bed that night thankful for the time we spent listening to our children when they were young. Open communication has made the teenage years so much fun. Our kids love talking to us, and we know it is a special gift that we wish all parents could enjoy.

Third, any type of hypocritical behavior will hinder relationship with our child. Actions speak louder than words. I have learned in my own parenting that my children may not always do what I say, but they consistently do what they see me do. Children are great students; unfortunately they study everything, not just what we want them to study. We will do great damage if we are telling our child not to lie, but they hear us lie to others on the telephone. The message, "Do as I say, not as I do" is often the nonarticulated message that our children pick up. This message will provoke your child to anger. They want to be proud of their parents. The truth "parents are the pride of their children" (Proverbs 17:6) is common across cultures. Children want their parents to be their role models. In order for that to happen, we do not need super powers, but we do need to avoid hypocrisy of every kind.

Don't worry that children never listen to you; worry that they are always watching you.
—Robert Fulghum,
All I Really Needed to Know I Learned in Kindergarten²

Fourth, not admitting mistakes or asking for forgiveness will frustrate your child. We need to ask forgiveness when we mess up. We teach our children how to apologize when they hurt someone or make mistakes. In the same way, we need to model this behavior for our children. This can happen naturally when we ask our children to forgive us when we make mistakes or lose our temper. Children are quick to learn and apologize from the way we apologize. Apologizing to our children does not make us submissive to them; rather, it models appropriate behavior (see Appendix C for more on asking forgiveness).

Fifth, constantly finding fault and nitpicking can lower children's self-esteem. Correcting our child's misbehavior is an important part of our parenting responsibility. Correcting misbehavior is different from being constantly critical, condemning, accusing, and judgmental. People often live up to the expectations of the authority figures in their lives. If your child believes that you think they are great, they will strive to meet your expectations. If they get the idea from you that they are lazy, messy, or dumb, they may just live up to that expectation.

One way to correct your child and still build their self-image is to emphasize their potential in the midst of correction. For example, you may say, "Johnny, I see that you didn't do your homework. I don't consider you a lazy boy, and I expect you not to be lazy with your homework." Spending a lot of time lecturing our children over every issue can be very counterproductive. It is important to save our sermons for serious corrections. Taking advantage of teaching moments when there is little crisis or tension is more effective than hot sermons. Remembering the phrase, "the more the words, the less the meaning" would help many of us as parents develop shorter and clearer instructions for our children.

Praise and encouragement are fundamental in building our children up. Encouragement is the building block for healthy self-esteem. Our children need to hear from us what they do right even more than what they are doing wrong. Every good behavior they choose to repeat because of our praise and encouragement takes time away from wrong behavior they could be doing. If our children are regularly hearing our praise for their good traits and behavior, they will think of themselves as good. When we need to discipline and correct bad behavior, it will be easier for them to receive such correction in a balanced way.

Sixth, failing to keep promises can cause children to loose trust. When we promise our children something, we intend to follow through. However, life happens, and that sometimes makes it impossible to follow through. It is important to ask our children to forgive us. Things go bad when breaking promises becomes a normal occurrence. A child will naturally begin to guard himself from further disappointment and hurt. Distrust of the parents' promises naturally results in the child's anger. The attitudes and feelings that grow in the heart of a child whose hopes are dashed on a consistent basis can be very harmful. These can include:

- Rejection/hurt feelings
- Discouragement/depression
- Loss of respect for parents
- Feeling unloved
- Bitterness growing into resentment
- Cynicism resulting in inability or unwillingness to trust

Over time, all of these can be healed by loving parenting. If left to grow, they will result in anger and rebellion.

Seventh, any form of abusing your children physically will produce lasting emotional damage. Our children need to be trained in appropriate behavior. This will require discipline for their wrong actions. This discipline can be administered lovingly or in anger. Loving, consistent discipline will produce good results, and angry, inconsistent discipline will provoke our children to anger. Here are some tips to help evaluate your discipline:

- Before disciplining our children, we should be sure that we have all the facts.

- We should make sure that our motives for disciplining are correct. Correct motives are to train our children in correct behavior so that they can be a blessing. Wrong motives for disciplining are because they embarrassed us or didn't meet our expectations. This latter discipline will be vindictive and abusive. Correct the behavior, but get your emotions under control so that you are disciplining for the correct reasons.

- We should never discipline when we are angry or our emotions are out of control. If we discipline in anger, we are likely to hurt our children physically or emotionally.

I will talk more on appropriate discipline in Chapter 25.

Eighth, comparing our children with their peers can also be very hurtful. In your marriage, think of the emotions that would come to mind if your spouse compared you to one of your peers. "Why didn't you get the raise like your friend, Bob?" "Your friend listens to his wife more than you listen to me." I know instinctively that these comments would not motivate me to be a better man or husband. They would only cause me to feel rejected, angry, and defensive. In the same way, my wife would be very upset if I asked her why she didn't treat me as well as her friend treats her husband or why she wasn't as thin as her friend. Either of these comments would produce negative feelings and result in conflict in our marriage. In a similar way, our children do not appreciate being compared with their peers. Choosing successful people for them to look up to and strive to emulate is different. It is wise to avoid comparing our children to their peers (favorably or unfavorably).

Ninth, we need to resist putting unrealistic expectations on our children. As an elementary education major in college, I was required to take a course called Early Childhood Development. This course discussed the developmental stages that all children go through. We should be careful not to place expectations on our children that they are incapable of performing developmentally. The challenge is that children reach different developmental stages based on their unique internal clock. That internal clock does not always relate directly to age. Some children mature faster than others and some slower. The parent who compares his children to others on a constant basis will just add unneeded stress to all their lives. Today this is especially challenging, as a result of how competitive education is within many countries of the world. First in the class today doesn't guarantee the best job or happy life tomorrow. If you give your child every lesson and all the best instruction, it does not guarantee they will be the first in their class. When our children do not measure up to the goals or expectations we place on them, we still need to encourage them. Life circumstances change expectations and help one clarify the important expectations from the unimportant.

> *Remembering that I'll be dead soon is the most important tool*
> *I've ever encountered to help me make the big choices in life.*
> *Because almost everything—all external expectations, all pride,*
> *all fear of embarrassment or failure—these things just fall away*
> *in the face of death, leaving only what is truly important.*
> —Steve Jobs

Setting goals for our children that reflect pride or unmet expectations from our own childhood will not help our children excel. Children are great learners, and we are their primary teachers. Every action, word, and breath we take becomes the textbooks of their lives. The following fable reminds us that we cannot expect our children to do what we ourselves are not doing.

The Young Crab and His Mother

"Why in the world do you walk sideways like that?" the mother crab said to her son. "Straight forward with your toes out is the way you should walk."

"Show me how to walk, Mother, so I can learn from you how to walk correctly."

So the old crab tried to walk straight ahead. But each time she tried, she walked sideways like her son. When she tried to turn out her toes, she fell straight on her nose.

The lesson learned: Do not expect to correct other's behavior unless you are able to set a good example yourself.

Application points:
- What did you learn from this chapter about exasperating children?
- What behaviors do you struggle with most?
- Who can objectively help you see and correct exasperating behaviors in your home?

Chapter 21

. . . .

Training in Wisdom

. . . .

A wise son brings joy to his father,
but a foolish son grief to his mother.

—Proverbs 10:1

The wise woman builds her house, but with her
own hands the foolish one tears hers down.

—Proverbs 14:1

As your child grows in maturity, it is important to train them in wisdom by teaching the reasons you tell them to do things. This is an important natural stage of maturity and can happen when children are walking in obedience. Once they have learned not to argue or talk back, they are ready to learn the reasons for these commands. This isn't inviting argument, but rather training in wisdom. Teaching the wisdom behind our decisions equips a child in how to make decisions on their own as they grow. The best time to discuss the reason behind a command is not at the time the command is given. Many parents allow debates to begin by allowing their children to ask why as a rule is applied. The first response following a command should be "yes, Mom" or "yes, Dad." This response should be followed by obedience to what was asked. It is important that our children learn to obey us without an argument promptly, without talking back. Inappropriate responses by children when asked to do something are:

- "But Mom, I'm not finished."
- "Ten more minutes. Pleeeeez!"
- "I'm not ready to go."
- "We just got here."

Breaking wrong responses is important in order to effectively train a child in wisdom. After a child obeys, there will be times when it is appropriate for us to explain why we asked them to do something. This pattern is important to establish when children are young. It is hard for an older child, who is used to parents persuading them into obedience, to break the habits of debating. However, it is still possible, so if your child is older, don't give up.

Once a child learns to obey parental authority in the home, move on to training them to be wise. As you see your child walking in obedience, it is appropriate to offer short reasons behind a command or request. Giving the reason should just be a reminder of a longer instruction regarding the moral behind such an action, such as teaching deference, respect for elderly, or patience.

Practically, these short instructions might sound something like this:
- "Joe, please share that toy for John's sake." (Deference)
- "Please be quiet. Uncle Bill is resting in the other room." (Respect)
- "Aunt Jane is really late, but it doesn't hurt us to wait." (Patience)

As my children respond appropriately in these situations, I make it a point to verbally thank them for their obedience. For example, I may say, "Thank you, Joe, for sharing your toy. I know you didn't want to, but you showed wonderful deference today." You could also say, "Johnny, I realize it was a small home and difficult to play quietly; however, your obedience allowed Uncle Bill to rest and that was a blessing and very respectful." Or, "Aunt Jane was embarrassed to be so late, but your positive attitudes helped her not feel so bad. Thanks for showing patience and being a blessing."

In this way, we have trained our children to be a blessing. Being a blessing is what they are supposed to do. Verbal appreciation is a positive reinforcement of the instructions given earlier. I still regularly teach my children appropriate behavior and discipline inappropriate behavior. I have found the more time I place on training, the less time I spend on disciplining. My favorite thing to do is reinforcing good behavior by words of appreciation and praise.

What can be done for an older child who is accustomed to arguing, debating, and complaining when asked to do something? Even though training will be more painful, it is definitely not too late for them. The issue at the core is training in self-denial. They can learn to say no to their own desires, feelings, and curiosity. To do this, they go back to the basic behavior of obeying without discussion. They obey whether they agree or disagree with what is being asked. This will be hard, and normally at their age, they could expect some short explanations. However, bad habits have to be broken before new ones can be learned.

Here are examples of what can be done for an older child:

- Begin by apologizing to them for failing to train them in some important areas that will affect their adult life.

- Explain that you are committed to their success and that for their maturity they will learn how to obey parental instructions without always knowing why.

- Make a set time for them to learn to obey promptly, respectfully, and completely. You could agree to two months or whatever time you feel could be effective.

- Explain that after this training time, they will be given short explanations for why they need to do something, but will not be allowed to show immature behavior (complaining, arguing, stalling).[1]

During this training time, they will respond with "Yes, Mom" or "Yes, Dad" when asked to do something. Then they will be expected to promptly obey unless it is an emergency. Examples of an emergency are when someone would be hurt by their obedience, the other parent has given an earlier contradicting command, or they cannot do what is asked of them for some reason beyond their control (a humorous but real possibility would be if they are asked to come but are tied up to a chair by a friend). As the time period comes to an end and they have shown self-control in obeying, then they will begin to receive explanations behind the commands. This will not reinstate arguing or debating, but will be short explanations reminding them of mature moral responses. If they have not demonstrated that they can use self-control and obey appropriately at the end of the designated time period, the time will be extended. If rebellion results during any time in the training, further privileges will be taken away. This may come across as harsh and feelings may be strained at times, but failure to train your child in self-control will lead to greater heartache throughout their adult life. The following story illustrates the importance of resisting greed and the importance that religious leaders play in our lives:

In the beautiful Himalayan foothills lived an order of Christian monks. They lived quiet lives of devotion and worship. This specific order loved to garden, and each year shared a majority of their harvest with the poor refugees who lived in the town below. The town was also a very prosperous farming community with a growing tourist industry. Its lush green fields were surrounded by majestic white-capped mountains. The soil of was good, but the real source of the monks' and farmers' success was the crystal-clear water that flowed down the mountain next to the monastery and into the village. The monks and farmers made small tributaries off the gentle mountain stream to water their gardens and fields.

The crystal-clear stream became so popular that a water-bottling facility was planning to move to the village. This exciting news came just before the annual meeting of the local town council, which was made up of leading farmers, merchants, and hotel owners. The agenda was dominated by the impact and potential benefits the new bottling factory would bring.

The Mayor said, "It's good for jobs, real-estate values, and local produce sales."

But farmers raised a concern regarding the volume of water needed for their fields and the factory. A good portion of the water flow was diverted toward the monastery. Since the monks had no representation on the council, it was decided that the monks would have to begin using other water sources that could supply their personal food needs, but unlikely much more.

One merchant argued, "With all the growth expected in the town, it would be better if the monks stopped supplying food for the poor refugees. They do have a negative effect on real-estate values."

Greed and unbridled ambition won over compassion that day, and the council agreed to redirect the spring. The leaders felt good about the decision, and all fall and winter plans moved ahead without a hitch. The monks accepted the news sadly and prayed for those who depended on their assistance. The town sent men to close off the tributaries that directed water toward the monastery. But the townspeople failed to realize that the monks not only used the water, but also helped regulate the flow of the stream, taking the brunt of the excess water during the highest flood season. Their diligence watching over the stream was never noticed. The monks warned the men closing up the tributaries, but their words fell on deaf ears.

When spring came, the town prepared for the crystal stream to begin its flow, the bottling plant to open, and the farmers to have a bumper crop. As expected, the stream flowed at twice its normal volume but brought with it soot and dirt churned up by the enlarged streambed. The farmers' fields were not prepared for the increased water flow. As a result their fields flooded, and the flood washed away a good portion of the rich topsoil. The new bottle factory found that its filters clogged with soot. The repairs to the damaged filters were not worth the investment, and the bottling plant closed and moved to another location.

The council realized their plans had ended in disaster. They admitted they had given into greed and shown a lack of self-control. They quickly reopened the tributaries leading to the monastery. The local economy took a severe hit that year, but the monks remained true to their religious vows and shared their produce with the town and saw that none went without food.

The town council recorded for future generations: "It has been our experience that when greed and lack of self-control remove the influence of religious leaders from a community, disaster will soon follow."

Parents, we are the protector of the spring for our children, teaching them self-control and helping them avoid greed and negative influences that will keep them from becoming loving, obedient children and someday, mature adults.

Application points:
- What did you learn from this chapter about training in wisdom?
- In what areas do you need to begin training your child in wisdom?
- When would you like to begin?

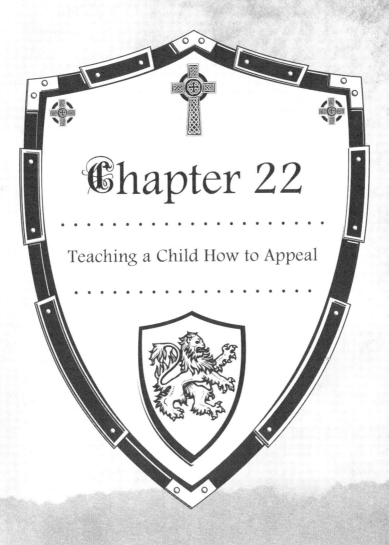

Chapter 22

Teaching a Child How to Appeal

I beseech you, in the bowels of Christ,
think it possible you may be mistaken.

—Oliver Cromwell

If my child began an appeal as Oliver Cromwell began his, I would be asking, "What body-snatching alien took over my child's mind?" However, learning how to effectively appeal is a skill useful in one's adult life and also important in childhood. When parenting, some of the quick answers I give to my children's requests are not always my final answer. In their first request, they are likely for the sake of time to leave out a lot of information that may affect my decision. In our home, we dealt with this issue by teaching our children the process of appeal. This was only introduced after we felt confident that our children had learned to obey without whining or complaining after being told only once.

Our goal was to teach our children how to ask us to reconsider our answer without showing disrespect. The process involves a few simple steps and situation-appropriate questions. Different parents may come up with what they want their children to say. For our family, we taught our children to simply say, "Can I ask a question?" if they wanted to appeal a decision. If we said yes, they then could ask a question and give the reason why they wanted to do something other than what they have been asked. For example, when we are ready to leave a friend's home and we tell them to stop playing because we are ready to leave, they could respond by saying, "Yes, Mom or Dad," followed by, "May I ask a question?" We say yes. Then they may ask, "We have a few minutes left before we finish this game, can I please finish it and then come?" If we say no, we expect immediate obedience with a good attitude. Or they may ask to go to a friend's house, and I say no without knowing all the facts. They say, "Can I ask a question?" I say yes, and they tell me that it's their friend's birthday party and their parents are planning a special surprise. In this process, I am glad for the extra information and change my answer because I see that it is important.

Some parents may ask their children to say, "May I make an appeal?" We liked "May I ask a question?" since it sounded less like a debate, but it basically meant that we were allowing them to appropriately make a respectful appeal. These appeals should not become a normal response each time you ask your children to do something that they don't want to do. The most common response should be "Yes, Mom" or "Yes, Dad." We also required our children to be in the process of obeying while they asked for permission to appeal. They were never allowed to ask why when asked to obey. When they asked for permission to appeal, we could give the reason for our response, but the burden of changing our mind rested on their appeal.

A respectful appeal will have the following characteristics:

- It will be stated as a question.
- It will be asked in a respectful tone of voice.
- It will not be a stalling tactic to delay obedience.
- It should be used occasionally when the child thinks they have a reasonable appeal.
- If the parent refuses to hear the appeal at that time, the child should obey immediately.

It might sound strange, but I remember teaching my oldest daughter as she was entering the teenage years about the importance of timing. She was getting in the habit of asking to do something or go someplace as soon as she entered the door from an event. It seemed that every activity was followed by a request for something else, without any gratitude being expressed over what she just finished. I let her know that if she asked me about sleeping over at a friend's house on her way in from a birthday party, she had less than a fifty-percent chance of getting a yes response. If she came in and showed appreciation for being allowed to attend the birthday party, then the following day asked about the sleepover, her chances of getting a yes increased to eighty percent or higher, depending on the circumstances. She learned this lesson quickly. I remember her asking me, "Dad, is this a good time to ask for permission to do something?" She came up with this question on her own, and it worked well for both of us. I felt she was more thankful, and she got more positive answers to her requests.

It is important that we do not kill our child's curiosity while teaching them obedience. Children are human sponges when they are young, and their curiosity is a gift to help them learn. Asking "Why?" should be something that we welcome when it is in relation to our child's curiosity. Why is the moon round? Why is the grass green? Why does Grandma snore when she sleeps? This type of "Why?" is not a defiant challenge to parental authority, but the natural curiosity of a child wanting to learn. I wish we all kept that curiosity longer. When we ask our children to pick up their toys and they say "Why?" it is unlikely that they really want to learn, but rather don't want to obey. This type of "Why?" should not be answered, but rather met with appropriate correction. The first time we hear our children say this, we just tell them that it's not appropriate for them to talk to us that way. If a verbal warning doesn't work, more discipline is required.

Teaching our children how to grow into mature knights and princesses is a task that will be learned, not in a moment, but over time. It will be learned by observation more than through instruction. Our behavior and example will be the greatest factor in training our children toward greatness. I would like to end this chapter with a challenging poem for both adult and child.

"If"
by Rudyard Kipling (1865–1936)

If you can keep your head when all about you
Are losing theirs and blaming it on you,
If you can trust yourself when all men doubt you,
But make allowance for their doubting too;
If you can wait and not be tired by waiting,
Or being lied about, don't deal in lies,
Or being hated don't give way to hating,
And yet don't look too good, nor talk too wise:

If you can dream—and not make dreams your master;
If you can think—and not make thoughts your aim,
If you can meet with Triumph and Disaster
And treat those two imposters just the same;

If you can bear to hear the truth you've spoken
Twisted by knaves to make a trap for fools,
Or watch the things you gave your life to, broken,
And stoop and build 'em up with worn-out tools:

If you can make one heap of all your winnings
And risk it on one turn of pitch-and-toss,
And lose, and start again at your beginnings
And never breathe a word about your loss;
If you can force your heart and nerve and sinew
To serve your turn long after they are gone,
And so hold on when there is nothing in you
Except the Will which says to them: "Hold on!"

If you can talk with crowds and keep your virtue,
Or walk with Kings—nor lose the common touch,
If neither foes nor loving friends can hurt you,
If all men count with you, but none too much;
If you can fill the unforgiving minute
With sixty seconds' worth of distance run,
Yours is the Earth and everything that's in it,
And—which is more—you'll be a Man, my son![2]

Application points:

- What did you learn from this chapter that you would like to teach your child?
- Which of the five characteristics of a respectful appeal would you like to teach your child?
- When would you like to begin teaching your child how to make a respectful appeal?

Chapter 23

. . . .

Overcoming Self-Indulgence
and Excuses Kids Make

. . . .

*Children today are tyrants. They contradict their parents,
they gobble their food, they terrorize their teachers.*

—Socrates, 426 BC

This sounds like something I overheard yesterday at the store. Child-training has always been fundamental to any society. Two thousand and four hundred years have passed since Socrates made this statement, and things haven't changed for the better. Parents are just as important today as they were then. Wise people learn from history in order to improve. One key to creating a happy, mature child is by helping them overcome a self-indulgent mind-set. Loving parents naturally want to shield their child from harmful situations and experiences that will cause them pain and hardship. However, sometimes in the attempt to protect our children from challenges, we can actually hinder their maturity. I am not saying we shouldn't protect our children. I am saying we need to create tasks and opportunities for them to grow that may not be enjoyable at first. It is also important for them to learn how to encourage themselves after a disappointment (like if a friend had to cancel a playtime or a toy breaks).

Many parents who desire to love and bless their children mistakenly foster self-indulgence. Here are the top fifteen tips for parents in teaching your child to overcome self-indulgent behavior:

Do's:

1. Let your child wait sometimes for things they want.

2. Require them to do daily tasks around the house. Housework is good for them and will give them a feeling of ownership and pride in the home. If you don't believe me, ask them to keep one area of the house clean (other than their own room). If you mess that

area up, they will need to clean it. Watch them encourage you to become less messy in the same way you have challenged them.

3. Give them structure in their day as to length of playtime, length of study, when to go to bed, etc.

4. Require them to fully obey you with a good attitude. Obedience without humility is passive rebellion and needs to receive a negative disciplinary consequence.

5. Be consistent in your discipline and expectations regarding their behavior and attitude.

6. Reward good behavior with verbal praise, greater responsibility, and increased privileges.

7. Set the example in everything you want them to learn. They watch even better than they listen. A parent who is self-indulgent, angry, and stubborn should not be surprised to see the same behavior in their child.

Don'ts:

1. Don't always provide activities for them when they are bored. Let them use their own imaginations at times and choose what to do.

2. Don't drop everything and run to them every time they call. Unless it is an emergency, let them come to you.

3. Don't allow them to put their hand on your mouth when they are ready to go and want you to stop talking. I saw this happen just today as a mother held a toddler. Consistently interrupting when you are talking to another adult is not acceptable. Let them know that you are having adult time and, unless it is an emergency, they need to wait until you are finished.

4. Don't allow them to interrupt your conversation. When they need your attention while you are talking, they can place their hand on your shoulder or leg. Then you can cover their hand with yours so they know you are aware of their desire to ask you a question. At a natural break in the conversation, you can ask what they want.

5. Don't allow them to complain about the food that is given them. They may request not to eat certain things and fill up on others. However, they don't need to comment on how horrible they feel about the food they dislike. Polite requests to abstain are not always disrespectful, and in some cases, the parents may have the same opinion. (This happens a lot with our family since we travel so often. Sometimes I just have to pass on some of the food that I see in restaurants, like chicken feet, fat cubes, or octopus tentacles. When nothing else looks good, our children have learned to fill up on rice or potatoes!)

6. Don't give them unlimited escape time, such as TV, video games, and hand-held games. In our home, we call it screen time, regardless of the media, and it is limited. You need to choose your limit and pay careful attention to content at all times.

7. Don't let them get away with messy rooms or messy play areas. After they are finished playing, require them to clean up. Small children will need help, but make sure they do their part. Train them to clean up after themselves when they are young and you will save yourself a ton of work and their future spouse will thank you.

8. Don't expect them to do something if you are modeling the opposite behavior.[1]

While we want our children to develop healthy self-esteem, we do not want to strengthen self-indulgent attitudes. Our goal is not that our children are constantly happy or entertained, but rather that they are growing in maturity. The above list is just a sample of parenting habits that can work for or against our best parenting efforts. Each parent should regularly assess their child-training habits and eliminate habits that encourage self-indulgent tendencies.

I vividly remember attending a conference where parents expressed a concern about raising their children. They feared that raising their children in a foreign country would cause their kids to be strange or weird when they returned to their home country for college. This fear resulted from stories of kids coming back to America with antisocial behavior and just being outright strange. I loved our speaker's answer. She said she had met some strange kids that had returned from overseas. She also had concluded the foreign environment must have encouraged or caused the development of this strange child. Her conclusion changed when she met the parents. She remarked that the kids where just as strange as their parents. Not more strange, and not less.

As daunting as it seems, we need to realize that our children learn mostly by watching our behavior. Our words and parenting practices will make a great difference, but the greatest effect will come simply from our relationship with our kids and who we are.

It is not a simple task to teach children to overcome self-indulgent behavior. They will apply many tactics to self-preserve an indulgent lifestyle. Our children will also come up with numerous excuses as to why you should allow them to continue in their self-indulgent behavior. All children are not "little Einsteins," but they all seem brilliant when it comes to getting what they want. Learning how to get their own way comes naturally for most children. Children dupe their parents on numerous occasions. In my home, I seem to be the one that gets tricked more than my wife. I am glad she is on my team because she saves me from committing to things that I shouldn't. I will be distracted, and the kids will come and nicely ask me something. I will say yes, and then I hear my wife say, "Do you know what you just agreed to?" I have no idea. So I quickly call them back and have them ask me again, this time with details. Most of the time the yes turns into a conditional yes based on their actions. Taking advantage of distracted parents is just one of the many ways our children learn to avoid responsibility.

Another tactic self-indulgent children use is projecting guilt on parents. Children can blame others for their wrong choices or even their parents for their lack of success. But the bottom line is their lack of success is mostly due to them seeking the most pleasurable path with the least amount of personal discomfort. Just yesterday I was with a good friend who had committed to help his daughter look at some very expensive private schools. Of the schools considered, one was out of their price range. The other two were more difficult and would require more work on the child's part. His child complained that she had such a poor family and because of her misfortune, she could not go to the school of her choice. I encouraged him that he was not poor and he was already providing his child with a wonderful opportunity for success. It was his daughter's responsibility to work hard in order to reach her goals. We all have limitations, and learning to overcome them is what makes us healthy, mature adults. I was happy to see that in a short period of time, his daughter went from complaining to being thankful.

When training children in obedience, you must persevere to victory. Every time a child receives what they desire through disobedient behavior, they have just been trained in how to get their way. Even if parents resist for hours and then finally give in, the child has just been taught that perseverance in disobedience will eventually win out.

Ten techniques kids use to avoid obedience include:

1. **Dividing and conquering**—getting Mom and Dad to disagree so the attention shifts off the issue of the child's disobedience to the parent's lack of unity.

2. **Avoiding**—children will avoid parents or other authorities when they are guilty of something. By avoiding, they hope their misbehavior will not be discovered. If you notice your child is avoiding you, you should make a point of checking in with them to make sure everything is okay.

3. **Rationalizing**—they push down their guilt by convincing themselves and others that their behavior was justified given their situation.

4. **Guilt-sharing**—one child may acknowledge what they did was wrong, but they were not the only ones who were doing it. They will seek to share the blame to minimize the fact that they made a choice to disobey and are personally responsible.

5. **Manipulating**—children learn what buttons to push very early. If they can use a parent's insecurities, they can often avoid receiving consequences for their misbehavior.

6. **Crying**—some children will fly into a fit of crying and wailing when they have been caught doing something wrong. The parents can be coerced into comforting the child instead of administering appropriate discipline.

7. **Whining**—children slowly wear down their parent's resistance with whining and complaining. Discipline is the best way to end a whining marathon.

8. **Patronizing**—this is where the child acts like they are listening and agreeing with what the parents are saying. In reality, they are just pretending to agree in order to minimize their consequences. Repeated disobedience over the same issue is a clue that a child may be outwardly pretending to comply.

9. **Embarrassing**—most children at one time or another make a scene in public where they think their parents will not dare hold them accountable. The wise parent still administers the appropriate discipline as close to the misbehavior as possible. Children need to learn they are accountable for their actions in public just as they are in their own home.

10. **Faking sickness**—my children developed stomachaches the moment they were asked to do some work. But their recovery was miraculously fast when it became time to play with a friend or eat some ice cream.[2]

Children naturally resort to the above behaviors and more in order to get what they want. If such behavior becomes a habit, the parent's lack of training has allowed it to be so. Children who are taught appropriate behavior learn responsibility for their actions. Most children naturally try things to get what they want, but if inappropriate behavior becomes a habit, the parents have trained their children in these bad habits. This was accomplished through the simple process of reinforcement and reward. The child, regardless of the scolding, was rewarded for his bad behavior. Most often the reward was getting the thing they wanted, even if it came after a long fight. Long battles of the will just train our children to persevere in bad behavior because in the end, parents will give in and they will win. A simple but challenging solution is: parents, train your children in right behavior and don't reward bad behavior.

A parent who perseveres in loving discipline will see good results over time. The following story illustrates how beneficial it can be to do the right thing. Once upon a time a wise king ruled over a peaceful kingdom. Though the kingdom was once strong and vibrant, the king noticed that years of prosperity were causing his people to become lethargic and discontented. So he came up with an idea to place a large boulder in the middle of the road. The nobles and wealthy citizens had to dismount or get out of their carriages in order to go around the bolder. The inconvenienced travelers complained openly and began quarrelling. Some even blamed the king for the problem. They complained that the king should do something about the disrepair of the roads.

Finally, a local peasant carrying a heavy load of vegetables for market came up to the boulder. Seeing a natural slope in the road, he figured he could roll it aside and help clear the road for others. Setting his own load down, he put his shoulder under the boulder and, easier than expected, sent the boulder rolling off the road and into the ditch. Returning to pick up his bundle of vegetables, he noticed a purse lying in the place where the boulder had sat. In the purse were a dozen gold coins and a note from the king: "This reward is for the person thoughtful enough to remove the boulder." That day the peasant learned that every obstacle is an opportunity to better one's situation.

Application points:

- What did you learn from this chapter that you would like to implement?
- What behaviors would you like to work on from the list of do's and don'ts?
- When will you start?

Chapter 24

. . . .

Training a Child's Appetite

. . . .

Unless someone like you cares a whole awful lot,
Nothing is going to get better. It's not.

—Dr. Seuss, *The Lorax*

A child's diet and physical health is a crucial part of parenting that needs to be taken seriously. In my early twenties, I worked in an inner-city rescue mission. Rescue missions provide food and shelter for those who are poor in the city. My job in the mission was to develop a youth program—providing activities and taking children to local churches and summer camping experiences. I had about thirty children in my program, and each week I visited these children in their homes. On one of those days, I visited the home of Johnny and Jill. Johnny was in seventh grade and Jill was in fifth. They were two of the happiest and most joyful children in my youth program. But both children faced the same challenge: obesity.

I arrived at their home on a late Saturday morning, while the family was having breakfast. All plates were covered with eggs, sausage, toast, and potatoes in large portions. Clearly, though the family was in a lower-rent district of the city, they were able to provide food for the family. I suspect this was how their parents showed their love and sent the message that "we have it good—just look at all you have to eat!" As I left that day, I thought Johnny and Jill would most likely be overweight their entire lives. Their parents, though well-meaning and loving, were creating eating habits that would directly affect their children's health and social acceptance all their lives.

Most adults and students away at college look forward to returning home for holidays. If you ask them what they are looking forward to, you may receive a variety of answers, but most of them will mention food. They may say they "can't wait to taste Ma's cooking" or they look forward to some local restaurant. They crave these foods because they were trained to eat them and therefore developed a taste for them. A child growing up in southern China may look forward to sweet fruits and cured sweet pork over rice. A boy growing up in an Alaskan tribe has learned to love fish with a large amount of fat. My children growing up in China have learned to love Chinese street food. Jian bing (egg pancake), ji dan bing (crispy pastry with egg and spicy sauce), and jiao zi (pot stickers) are all things I had no desire for when I was a child. I mention these as examples in order to highlight the fact that children learn to love the foods they are trained to eat from childhood.

Parents can choose to make nutritious foods that are good for health and building the body. If they do this, the child will have healthy eating habits to support a healthy life. If children are given foods to satisfy their hunger that are not good for health or in quantities that lead to obesity, it stands to reason that as an adult the child will develop habits that support an unhealthy life.

Giving in to the child's every desire is not responsible parenting. It will actually produce a very insecure and stressful child. You may have heard parents say: "but he only likes to eat sweets and bread, what can I do?" The more the parents give in to the child's unhealthy eating habits, the more powerful those habits become. In the same way, the more the parents require the child to eat healthy food, the more eating healthy will become a lifestyle. When given the choice, a child will usually choose sweets over healthy food, unless he or she has learned to enjoy the healthy feeling that results from nutritious food. Sweets will still be desired, but much more so in moderation.

I have come to learn that children love routine. People, children in particular, are creatures of habit. Routine and consistency give children a sense of security. Children will learn habits from their parents. If parents have bad eating habits, in most cases children will also develop bad eating habits. Discipline in the area of food is difficult, but it is very important. If your personal health isn't motivating enough for developing healthy eating habits, maybe your child's health will be the motivation you need. Kids will naturally crave healthy food just as they crave cookies and candy once they are trained in healthy eating. Once good eating habits become routine, they will be easy to maintain.

Hunger will drive a child to desire foods that are good for them if unhealthy foods are not an option. In a child's early years, the child is not to blame if he develops unhealthy eating habits; the fault lies with the parents or grandparents. Parents control the child's diet. Why wouldn't parents train their children in healthy eating habits? I am sure all families have their own excuses, but these are some of the shortcomings our family regularly fights to overcome:

- We are too tired at mealtime to make our kids eat what they don't want to eat. We choose less stress in the short-term, even though we know we will have to deal with it later.

- Some of our children gag and vomit easily, and as a result it is difficult to get them to eat foods they don't like.

- The biggest challenge is eating healthy foods myself (Carolyn is better than me). It is very hard to teach my children healthy eating habits when I don't have them.

Here are some of the reasons to overcome our child's excuses and train them in good eating habits:

- Food is one of the first places our children express their selfish wills. It is our first opportunity to teach them to obey even when they would rather not.

- By requiring our kids to eat different foods, they can avoid becoming picky eaters. Picky eaters have a hard time enjoying travel or even eating out at people's homes. To not eat what is prepared for you when you are guests in another's home is rude. Parents can save their children this embarrassment by helping them learn to eat a variety of good foods.

- Eating foods they don't like helps children learn to do hard things. If they can learn to eat things they don't like because it is good for them, they can also take on hard tasks in life and at their jobs that will be good for their future.[1]

When my siblings and I were young, my parents didn't always make us eat the food that was set before us at dinnertime. We were not allowed to complain, but we could choose to not eat. However, when the rest of the family was enjoying a snack later in the evening, my unfinished food was still waiting for me on the same plate on which it was served. It naturally tasted worse cold than hot, but that was what I had to eat before I could enjoy anything else. In this way, we learned to eat what was placed before us or go hungry. Hunger has a way of making once intolerable food tolerable.

Training a child's eating habits is by no means easy. Very few worthwhile things in life are easy. The easy thing is to give a child what he wants to eat when he wants to eat it. In this way, a child will be satisfied and parents can enjoy some peace. However, this type of peace comes at a great cost and a great disservice to the child's future success and happiness. The primary and obvious consequences of unhealthy eating habits are low energy, difficulty concentrating, obesity, and poor health.

One afternoon my wife was helping our youngest son with schoolwork. Like any day as a parent, some days are great, others are okay, and some have us pulling our hair and questioning why God didn't just have us reproduce adults. This was one of the hair-loss weeks. Our ten-year-old just couldn't sit still, nor could he concentrate on his work. He was in tears, and my wife was frustrated. Then she realized each morning of that week we had allowed him to get his own breakfast, and he had prepared sugary cereal. The next day she made him eggs and toast, and he was a different boy (he had better concentration, self-control over his emotions, and an overall happier disposition). Avoiding a high-sugar breakfast might seem obvious to many, but the importance had slipped from our minds. Diet will have a direct effect on your child's academic performance. Healthy eating affects adults and children alike.

In my own family, we have had some weight challenges. My son Timothy started to gain a lot of weight at age ten and soon became noticeably overweight. During his yearly checkups, for two years in a row, the doctor suggested he needed to lose weight to be in his appropriate weight category. I remember when Timothy was twelve and increasingly overweight, the doctor challenged us as parents, saying that typically overweight children become overweight adults. Being aware of the many social and health challenges that come from being overweight, we were concerned and worked to establish better eating habits and more regular exercise for the entire family. We know these habits will continue to serve him in his future. Fortunately for Timothy, his weight problem disappeared with puberty. He inherited height from my side of the family, and between the ages of twelve and fourteen, his weight stayed the same but he grew at least one foot in height. We watched that pudgy body transform into a tall, muscular six-foot-one teenager.

Reaching a healthy weight should be the goal. A healthy weight for yourself or your children should not be determined by looking at television or magazine models. Many models are so thin that they are actually unhealthy. Our son Timothy is a perfect example. We were concerned and worked hard to teach him good eating habits. As a result, he developed good eating habits, but remained on the chunky side until he hit puberty. Some kids are just husky around eleven to thirteen years of age. Don't stop them from eating, but teach them good eating habits.

The Boy and the Jar of Nuts
from *The Book of Virtues*
by Aesop

A little boy once found a jar of nuts on the table.

I would like some of these nuts, he thought. *I'm sure Mother would give them to me if she were here. I'll take a big handful.*

So he reached into the jar and grabbed as many as he could hold. But when he tried to pull his hand out, he found the neck of the jar was too small. His hand was stuck, but he did not want to drop any of the nuts.

He tried again and again, but he couldn't get the whole handful out. At last he began to cry.

176

Just then his mother came into the room. "What's the matter?" she asked.

"I can't take this handful of nuts out of the jar," sobbed the boy.

"Well, don't be so greedy," his mother replied. "Just take two or three, and you'll have no trouble getting your hand out."

"How easy that was," said the boy as he left the table. "I might have thought of that myself."

The moral: Self control and moderation will produce better results than taking too much at one time.

Teaching our children self-control will allow them to enjoy many successes in life. On the flip side, lack of self-control in the area of diet will hinder our children in many aspects of life.

Application points:
- What did you learn from this chapter about health that you would like to implement?
- Do you need to make any changes in your family regarding diet and exercise?
- If so, what changes would you like to make and when will you start?
- Who do you need to support and encourage you as you implement these changes?

Chapter 25

. . . .

Dealing with Rebellion

. . . .

Never give in, never give in, never, never, never—in nothing, great or small, large or petty—never give in except to convictions of honor and good sense.

—Winston Churchill[1]

Dealing with rebellion is like waging war. It will take a great amount of perseverance, but our children need us to win the battle. As you begin to regain authority in your home, you will weed out bad behavior just as you pull weeds and plant new behavior. In the weeding process, one weed is pulled out, just to be replaced by another weed that is not as obvious as the first. Rebellion can be the same; when dealing with active rebellion, one needs to be careful it is not replaced with passive rebellion.

Open or active rebellion is one of the first behaviors most parents are quick to address. Active, willful rebellion comes in many forms and if left to mature, will reap terrible consequences for your child's adult life. Active rebellion can be defined as consciously disobeying an established rule or command. For example, if you say to your child, "David, come here" and he doesn't, "don't touch that" and they do—these are all examples of active rebellion in younger children. Older children will likely add disrespectful responses.

Other forms of active rebellion include:

- Sassing, arguing, and complaining
- Throwing temper tantrums and hitting
- Ignoring instructions
- Resisting parent-initiated action[2]

These types of behavior are easy to see and to identify as behavior that must be eliminated and replaced with appropriate behavior.

Passive rebellion is another type of rebellion that is more subtle and harder to see, but equally dangerous. We may train our children to overcome active rebellion only to have it replaced by passive rebellion. This is not an acceptable compromise. Passive rebellion is often unplanned by the child. Children are sometimes unaware that they are rebelling and disobeying their parents. Many parents tolerate a great deal of passive rebellion.

Some examples of passive rebellion include:

- Walking away while being spoken to
- Obeying with a bad attitude
- Constant forgetfulness
- Doing what is asked, but not the way they know it should be done
- Breaking understood but unspoken rules
- Reactive lying or embellishing a story to escape punishment[3]

Ways to deal with rebellion in children

We were overseas when we started our parenting. As a result, we didn't have our parents or extended family nearby for advice. However, we were blessed with older friends living in Asia who shared their wisdom and experience. I remember one such couple helping us when we were dealing with difficulties raising our young children. They said, "Don't worry about fixing everything all at once. Work on eliminating one bad behavior or habit at a time." This didn't mean that we ignored open rebellion or inappropriate behavior. What it did mean was we focused on a certain action that was not appropriate and specifically worked on eliminating the bad behavior and training in the appropriate behavior. This approach required time and consistency, but it made the whole parenting process less overwhelming. I share this to remind you that parenting isn't a sprint, but a marathon.

One common mistake when seeking to weed out rebellious behavior includes warning without follow through. This will cause a child to ignore a parent's word. When dealing with rebellion, you must discipline rather than just warn. As parents, we usually warn our children in the hope that the warning itself will be enough to correct the behavior. This may work when our children are in the habit of obeying—they only need to be reminded that disobedience and rebellion is still not acceptable. However, when we warn of discipline, we should make good on our word and follow through. Early in a child's life they can be clearly trained in obedience. As they grow older, continue to train them in appropriate behavior in different environments. Things do change as they get older, but the basic principle of respect and obedience will lay a wonderful foundation in which to train your child to maturity.

Another common mistake involves regularly disciplining while angry. Disciplining while angry can damage a child emotionally. Parents are more likely to administer inappropriate or excessive discipline when they are angry. It is normal to be angry when children are in need of discipline. However, let your anger pass, and discipline for the correct reason. When you discipline in anger, you are not correcting the problem. Rather, you are creating deeper and longer-lasting problems.

Scolding in anger is another form of ineffective discipline. "Do not let any unwholesome talk come out of your mouths, but only what is helpful for building others up according to their needs, that it may benefit those who listen" (Ephesians 4:29). The Greek word in this quote regarding scolding literally means "to snort with anger." H. Clay Trumbull in his book *Hints on Child Training* states:

> To "scold" is to assail or revile with boisterous speech. The word itself seems to have a primary meaning akin to that of barking or howling. Scolding is always an expression of a bad spirit and of a loss of temper... The essence of the scolding is in the multiplication of hot words in expression of strong feelings that, while eminently natural, ought to be held in better control.[4]

Scolding our children while angry may produce short-term results, but models behavior that our children should not repeat. Exercising self-control and giving appropriate consequences set a much better example.

Administering inconsistent discipline is very hard on children. Inconsistent discipline is often administered in two forms. One involves inconsistencies between mother and father. One parent may be very strict while the other is more lenient. One behavior may be acceptable with Dad and not acceptable with Mom. It would be better for parents to adjust their standards so that parents can train in a united effort. Unified parents with consistent rules regarding behavior and consequences create clear expectations of behavior for a child to follow. Without a united approach, the child is prone to look for ways to weaken parents' resolve. The time it takes for parents to talk through and agree on what is acceptable behavior and consequences for misbehavior will reap wonderful results in child-training.

The second common mistake parents make also deals with inconsistencies. One day a certain behavior is severely punished, the next day it is overlooked. Our children are trying to figure out their world, and the more consistent we can be in our training, the faster they will be able to please us and behave appropriately. As children grow and change, they need to be regularly reminded of what behavior is appropriate for each season of life.

Disciplining rebellion

Each child is different and will respond differently to various types of discipline. Here are a number of possible disciplines for you to choose from, as well as some basic principles regarding discipline.

Our children have privileges they most likely think of as rights. I remember telling my children that when they were obedient, I would work to give them as many privileges and freedoms as they could handle (I wanted to start with the positive). I went on to say that if they chose to disobey or proved themselves untrustworthy, they would be amazed at how little freedom they would have. They smiled, but clearly understood the message.

I remember traveling in our car on long trips and disciplining as we traveled. Our children would get too loud or just become obnoxious in their teasing of each other, mostly out of boredom. At such times, I would demand silence usually from the child who was causing the most trouble. I would remind them that talking in our home is a privilege. I remember one time when traveling in the car that Timothy lost that privilege to talk. About five minutes later I told Timothy that he could talk again, and he let out a big sigh as if I had forced him to hold his breath the whole time. This example may sound simplistic, but it illustrates that something as basic as talking is a privilege that can be used to train our children in appropriate behavior.

In the training process, children should be told in advance, whenever possible, the type of discipline they can expect when they disobey. In this way, the child is choosing by their actions to receive discipline, and you are being true to your word when you administer it. This creates clear boundaries in which children can securely live.

Spanking on the bottom is another form of discipline that is common for younger children. It should always be done when the parents are under control and not angry. It should preferably not be done with the hand. In our home, we used a wooden spoon, which is also what my parents spanked me with as a child. It should be hard enough to sting but not so hard that it leaves a bruise. One to three swats usually does the trick and produces tears and repentance in younger children.

Many parents struggle with the issue of spanking. Some say it is cruel and will promote violence in a child. I am sure there are homes where parents spank and the children grow up violent, but in these cases I would argue that parents likely spanked out of anger or in excess. When parents choose not to spank, they usually are left with the following ineffective forms of discipline that seldom work for young children: bribing, threatening, reasoning, and appealing to their emotions. I have used all of these on occasion and found them to be short-term solutions or totally ineffective. Spanking proved to be the most loving form of discipline that corrected misbehavior and allowed our children to be joyful and kind to one another.

In our home, by the time our children were between five and eight years old, we no longer spanked. By the age of five, we began to use loss of privileges as a deterrent to active and passive rebellion. Again, letting children know in advance whenever possible what consequence they will receive for disobedience is important. My children, being very creative, sometimes disobeyed in areas I hadn't imagined. In such cases, I disciplined in proportion to the offense. Some possible forms of discipline include loss of privileges and restoring damage done. For example:

1. Using privileges as discipline.

- If they are reckless with a bike or toy, they lose it for a season.

- Toys left out and not put away are taken away for a period of time.

- Clothes not put away can also be taken away or a child can be required to put away additional clothing that belongs to parents. This can help them be thankful for all the years you put their things away when they were younger.

- If lazy with chores, they receive extra chores.

- If they are ungrateful, they lose a privilege.

- If they talk back when asked to do something, they get more of what they don't want to do.

- If they say they are bored, they get work to help overcome their boredom. This has worked wonders in our home. Our children soon eliminated "I'm bored" from their vocabulary and learned to be creative in filling their time.

- If they eat dinner too slowly or complain about what is served, you tell them dinner is over and feed it to them the next morning for breakfast. If they want a snack later that night, cold leftover dinner is their only option. (This worked on me when I was growing up. My parents found it amazingly successful.)

2. Restoring damage done as discipline.

- Restitution. Children should be required to pay for things they destroy or break when disobedient. When it involves breaking rules set by others, they should apologize to the person whose rules they violated. I still remember our father forcing my brother and me to apologize to a hotel manager when we snuck out at night and swam in the pool after the pool closed. My dad also grounded us to our room for sneaking out, but I most remember being terrified about apologizing to another adult for breaking their rules. This is a practice I continued with my own children. It has proven to be a very effective deterrent to disobedience.

- Repair. If they break it, they need to fix or replace it with their own time or money. Younger children without money should be required to help fix or watch the process of fixing what they broke. By watching the process, they can still see the effect of their destructive or careless behavior. I am not talking about clumsiness. Children bump into things and drop things accidentally and should not receive discipline unless it involves disobedience. They can still repair any damage done, but should not be made to feel shamed. The time spent fixing something is always a good reminder to be more careful next time.

- Restoration. If your children make a mess, they clean it up. Younger children may need help, but they participate to the point that stretches their comfort level.[5]

If repeated acts of disobedience increase, the severity of the discipline should increase proportionately. They obviously are choosing rebellion. Whenever I discipline my children, I remind them they make choices that can bring good or unpleasant results. Children will often see themselves as victims of their own impulses or external temptations. By reminding them that they made a choice, they learn they have the power to make the correct choice. If they choose wisely, they will reap positive results. I like the exhortation from the writer of Hebrews 12:11: "No discipline seems pleasant at the time, but painful. Later on, however, it produces a harvest of righteousness and peace for those who have been trained by it."

Application points:

- What did you learn from this chapter about rebellion?
- What rebellious behaviors are present in your home?
- What are the first rebellious behaviors you would like to focus on correcting?

Chapter 26

. . . .

A Grandparent's Vital Role

. . . .

We're all of us tiny drops in a vast ocean,
but some of them sparkle.

—King Arthur in *Camelot*

Grandparents understand the span of one's life is like a drop in the bucket, whose ripples will soon be stilled and will vanish from human sight. The way to sparkle and sparkle is to leave behind loving memories of a life shared with family—especially grandchildren.

As soon as you bring the first grandchild into the world, you give your parents new titles of grandma and grandpa. Your child becomes part of an extended family that can offer security and belonging. Each family is different with a variety of traditions and history. Your personal family history will, to a great extent, affect the role grandparents will have in your child's life. If your relationship with your parents is strong, having a child will likely further strengthen that relationship. If strained, a child presents a new opportunity to bring healing and restoration.

The challenge of raising children in these difficult times requires us to take advantage of all the resources available. Grandparents are a natural place to turn. How you plan to tap into their knowledge and experience will depend on a lot of factors. In the best situations, grandparents provide nurturing care, maturity, experience, stability, perspective, and unconditional love. In situations where one parent is absent permanently or for a time, grandparents can fill in for the missing male or female role model. Grandparents can also bring love, purpose, energy, and laughter. As parents, we need to be intentional in how we involve our own parents in our child's life. Family relationships are not always easy, but a strong family is a powerful force in any child's life. Help your child enjoy the power of a strong family. The rest of this chapter as well as the next two chapters are written specifically to the grandparents.

Relevant parenting books may be in short supply today, but resources encouraging grandparents are almost nonexistent. There is an expectation that grandparenting should come naturally since grandparents have already raised their children. However, grandparenting comes with a new set of challenges and opportunities much different from parenting. For starters, you don't get to choose when you become grandparents. It just happens when your little baby has a baby, and presto—your world changes. Your title changes, and you ask yourself, "How can someone as young as me be a grandparent?" Then you look in the mirror and in spite of how young you feel on the inside, you realize that grandparenting is your new season of life. You are forced to face the reality of your age. As a grandparent, you now take your place in your family as the older generation. If you are like most, you feel that parenting flew by incredibly fast and it is hard to believe that your little son or daughter has a family of their own. Just as parenting went by so quickly, I can guarantee that grandparenting will go by just as fast, if not faster. It is a profound and exciting time, but it also comes with many new challenges. In order not to miss the special moments, you need to prepare and plan. For new grandparents and those who are already grandparents, the following advice may inspire you to change or adjust how you relate to your grandchildren. Lets begin by talking about planning.

Planning is important because your child's growing family needs your influence in order to succeed in these challenging times. Your grandchild also needs the love, wisdom, and perspective that you have developed over the years. Young couples face many relational and financial pressures, as well as the pressure of your grandchild's education. Your grandchild will grow up in a fast-paced world that makes your world seem simple and peaceful in comparison. Such a big opportunity deserves some thought and planning. What type of relationship do you hope to have with your grandchild? How will you achieve your goal? Here are some questions you might want to ask yourself:

- What are your child's and his/her new family's expectations of you?

- How much time can you realistically commit?

- Will you need to adjust your work to free up more time or set aside financial resources to assist the family?

- What do you hope to pass on to your grandchild in the areas of faith, values, and culture? (See Appendix D for more helpful questions.)

By answering some of these questions, you can begin developing ways to accomplish your goal. Thinking before you act is so important as you begin this role. Parents are naturally insecure and unprepared for the role of parenting. They do need your help and support; however, if they feel judged by you rather than supported, you may find yourself shut out when you want to be invited in. A simple comment like "the baby doesn't have warm enough clothes" can be taken as criticism and be hurtful to a new mother. Grandparenting is not a time to say whatever you think because you are the oldest member of the family. It is a time to be tactful and resourceful.

Most people around the world are experiencing increased life expectancy. I recently read that age sixty is the new forty. Grandparents today don't think of themselves as old, simply because most of them are not that old—at least not in comparison to how long most of them will live. Today's grandparents are the best educated, most active, and youngest "older" generation that has ever lived. In spite of financial challenges, grandparents have more discretionary income than their parents could have ever imagined. Because people are living longer, more are becoming grandparents. This new generation of grandparents needs to take the time to consider carefully the influence they hope to have. Make a plan for your role of grandparenting since you may be at it longer than you think!

The best-laid plan will not go very far if you can't have access to your grandkids because of broken relationships with children and their spouses. If your relationship with your child is strained, now is a time to pursue a fresh start. Forgiveness will have to be extended. Trust will need to be rebuilt, but grandchildren create a natural opportunity to improve the relationship. Don't miss the opportunity to rebuild or to continue because of repeat hurtful behaviors. All your great experience and wisdom will accomplish little if your words and actions offend and make the parent feel insecure. Giving advice that can be received is a real art. Anyone can say what he or she thinks, but to say it in a way that it will be helpful is a learned skill.

> *The true secret of giving advice is, after you have given it*
> *honestly, to be perfectly indifferent whether it is taken or not*
> *and never persist in trying to set people right.*
> —John Rosemond

> *Everyone is entitled to my opinion.*
> —Yogi Berra

You can choose which of the above pieces of advice will produce the best results. Let me end this chapter with relational advice. The best intentions will not get you very far if you are not allowed into your grandchild's life because of hurt relationships with your children or their spouses. Ask yourself, "What does this family need from me that I can give that will be received as a blessing and not an intrusion? What steps do I need to take to restore or protect the future of my relationship with my family?" Family relationships are very complicated, largely because they are so important. Do the hard work of repairing broken relationships. If relationships are good, don't take them for granted; protect them and work hard to maintain good relationships because your grandkids need you. When it comes to grandkids, life gets much simpler, and grandkids naturally desire to love and be loved by their grandparents. We will all leave a legacy. What will yours be?

Application points:
- What did you learn from this chapter about grandparenting?
- How could you begin planning in order to maximize your years as a grandparent?
- Who do you know that could help support you in your role as grandparents?
- For parents, what do you need to do in order to best involve your parents in your child's life?

Chapter 27

. . . .

The Grandparents' Blessings

. . . .

You must know that there is nothing higher and stronger and more wholesome and good for life in the future than some good memory, especially a memory of childhood, of home.

—Fyodor Dostoyevsky, *The Brothers Karamazov*

Grandparents are perfectly positioned to pass on blessings to their grandkids and to begin their good memories. Words are powerful, and a well-thought-out blessing can help grandkids feel and act as knights or princesses. As a grandparent, you have a few wonderful gifts with which to bless your grandchildren. The three most important gifts are love, support, and perspective.

I know my grandparents played a special part in making me feel loved and a part of something special. As a young boy, my parents left me with my grandpa and grandma Buck for some of the summer. Their names were Clair and Bill Lawry. We kids called them "Grampa and Gramma Buck" because Grandpa loved to hunt and shot a buck (a male deer) almost every year. I still remember how special I felt when Grandpa called me his "right-hand man." I have talked to many college students and young adults who say their grandparents were the most influential people in their lives. Others refer to the life of their grandparents as the inspiration for them to succeed and to develop a loving relationship with God. For many families, grandparents are the anchors that keep life stable during turbulent times.

Fred Rogers, host of the Mister Rogers' Neighborhood children's television program, recalled the advice of his grandfather: "Freddie," his grandfather said, "you make my day very special."[1] Fred Rogers touched millions of children with his grandfather's special blessing, using that phrase as a hallmark of his television show.

With extended time, grandparents can offer the blessing of support. Today's world will not naturally groom your grandchildren to become knights or princesses; rather, your grandchild is entering a world filled with many traps and snares. Your help and support is more needed than ever. Just a few short generations ago, people lived close to their extended family, moms stayed home, and grandparents played a natural role in the family. Today many, if not most, moms are in the workforce. Children go to daycare and kindergarten at a young age. The divorce rate is above fifty percent in some countries and rising in most.

When mom and dad get divorced, grandparents and grandchildren share a common pain. They both ask, "Was it something I did or didn't do?" and "Can I still do anything to bring them back together?" Children whose parents are divorced or separated may seek special help from grandparents. Questions dealing with forgiveness, remarriage, and communication will be very difficult for children to process on their own. In these situations, grandparents can be especially helpful if children are open to their support. These common hurts and heart-searching questions can create a special bond between grandparent and grandchild.

These situations and many more make raising healthy, successful children into knights and princesses a huge challenge. Grandparents can play a natural part in helping children navigate through these issues. Grandparents that are engaged in the family also become symbols of emotional and structural security. Through practical help, and sometimes financial help, they can offer the family increased economic stability. They also provide emotional stability by being present and offering a listening ear and unconditional love.

> *If nothing is going well, call your grandfather or grandmother.*
> —Italian proverb

Growing up, I remember some great times when our larger Foster family gatherings included grandparents as well as aunts, uncles, and cousins. These family gatherings gave me a broader perspective of who I was and how I fit into the world. It also gave me a sense of security by being connected to a larger extended-family structure. Feeling part of a good family makes a child feel safe and protected from danger. Having a supportive family to return to allows children to take chances and to try new things because they know if they fail or fall down, their family will be there to help pick them up. Grandparents play a central role in providing perspective that creates security and stability for the family.

Time is one of the greatest gifts that can ever be given. Taking time to listen to your grandchildren will open up the opportunity for you to share your faith, values, and traditions. In this fast-moving world, children need to see they are valued, and focused time spent with them can help them feel important. Grandparents can offer so much emotional stability by listening and offering unconditional love. A close relationship between grandchildren and grandparents often begins just by spending time together.

Perspective is also gained by learning about family traditions and values. Traditions and family values can give grandchildren a sense of being rooted and stable. Participating in family traditions is often the most natural way for grandchildren to learn. Values can transfer naturally by telling stories from your past while walking in the park or sitting on the slide. By telling stories about when you were young, grandchildren will be able to identify and see you in a new way. Including the spiritual elements as well as the lessons learned while growing up can build deep memories. If attention span hinders you from finishing a particular story, finish it at another moment in the day. You may not get a lot of response, but your stories will lay a deep foundation in your grandchild's life and memories.

In addition to telling stories, the greatest way to teach your grandchild values and faith is by modeling a moral and faith-filled life. Children study the actions of their grandparents just as they study their parents. Taking time to explain the meaning behind your actions is also important for children of all ages. Don't assume they just know. For example, if you pray in the morning before you start your day, tell your grandchild why you pray and what difference it has had on your life through the years.

Family holidays are also great opportunities to teach values to grandchildren. Most holidays have historical foundations. Make sure your grandchildren know the meaning behind your holiday traditions. The same holds true for unique family foods or activities—take the time to tell the story. Stories and history give deeper understanding and insight to family traditions.

Stories of your successes and failures from your past also play a special role in your grandchild's life. Your grandchild will likely use the stories you share to brag to others or to explain why their family is special. Children naturally want to boast about their parents' and grandparents' accomplishments. It adds to their feeling of self-worth and can help build their self-esteem. You don't have be the CEO of a large company or a famous celebrity; children will brag about the fact that their grandpa takes them to the park and to McDonald's or that their grandma plays games with them and makes the best desserts in the whole wide world. Take the time to share your life with your grandchildren so they can be proud of you. Your gifts of love, support, and perspective will make a wonderful difference in your grandchild's life.

> *Since my youth, O God, you have taught me, and to this day*
> *I declare your marvelous deeds. Even when I am old and*
> *gray, do not forsake me, O God, till I declare your power to*
> *the next generation, your might to all who are to come.*
> —Psalm 71:17–18

Your grandchildren will be truly blessed as you share your love, support, and perspective. By sharing these gifts, your words and blessings over them will have a deep and profound impact on their lives. Take the time to speak blessings over your grandchild.

Let me end this chapter by sharing a blessing I heard just the other day that gave me a warm feeling. It sounds better if you read it with an Irish accent.

> May the road rise up to meet you.
> May the wind always be at your back.
> May the sun shine warm upon your face,
> and rains fall soft upon your fields.
> And until we meet again,
> May God hold you in the palm of his hand.
> —An Old Irish Blessing

Application points:

- What did you learn from this chapter that you would like to implement?
- What words of blessing would you like to begin speaking to your grandchildren?
- For parents, what words of blessing would you like to begin speaking to your child?
- When would you like to start?

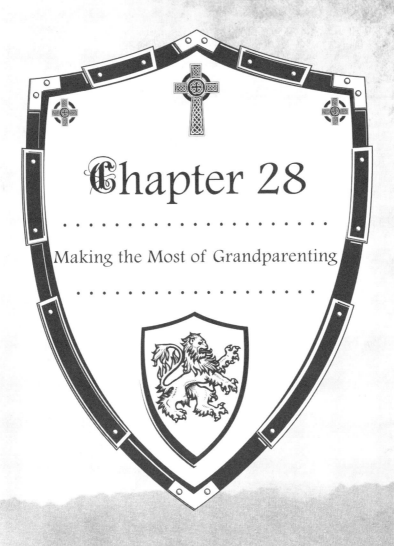

Chapter 28

Making the Most of Grandparenting

*If I had known how much fun grandchildren were,
I'd have had them first.*

—Author Unknown

Becoming a grandparent is a major transition in a person's life, so how can you celebrate and make that transition meaningful? Once a pregnancy is announced, most of the attention will be on the expectant mother and new baby. At the same time, this new grandchild is the beginning of a new stage of life for you as the grandparent. It is appropriate to celebrate such a meaningful event. Some type of ritual or ceremony should accompany this rite of passage. When such a change goes uncelebrated, the meaning can be devalued and unnoticed. I am not suggesting that you wait for someone else to throw you a party or bring you gifts. I am suggesting you do something meaningful for you to mark this major transition in your life. Some suggested ceremonies or events to mark this historic transition could include:

- Planning a meal with other close friends who are already grandparents and talking about your feelings regarding grandparenting.

- Buying some gifts like toys, picture frames, albums, or children's books. They don't have to be expensive gifts but rather gifts that will help you enjoy special times with your grandchild.

- Marking this special event by planting a tree so you can watch it grow as your grandchild grows.

- Planning a private ritual, like a special dinner with your spouse, to celebrate.

Just as you celebrate this new season of your life, take the time to recognize your friends who are beginning the wonderful challenges of being first-time grandparents. At each stage of life, people are searching for significance. Instead of trying to fill your life with things to make you feel significant, fill your life with significant people and relationships. Your grandchildren are the most significant people I can think of.

Now that you are a new grandparent, how are you going to make the most of it? In the last chapter we discussed passing on faith, values, and traditions. This chapter will focus on other aspects of grandparenting, such as gift giving, spending time reading, and keeping in touch from a distance. Let us begin by looking at gift giving.

Gift giving usually begins even before the first grandchild is born. Just the announcement of a potential grandchild opens up whole new areas of shopping that were irrelevant just days before. Now toys, building blocks, baby clothes, cribs, and baby strollers are potential purchases. What an exciting and refreshing change from paying thousands of dollars in college tuition, insurance, and car and house payments! Now you can bring a child joy through the gift of a new toy or a colorful picture book. Gift giving provides an avenue for grandparents to spoil their grandchildren. In the Old Testament of the Bible it says, "A gift opens the way for the giver and ushers him into the presence of the great" (Proverbs 18:16). As a grandparent, is there any greater privilege than to be ushered into the presence of your grandchild through a gift?

When selecting gifts for your grandchild, you will want to think of what message you hope to convey. For example, do you want your gift to:

- Stimulate imagination?
- Teach a useful skill?
- Introduce a new experience?
- Be a practical help?
- Bring excitement and delight?
- Develop fine motor skills?
- Deepen your relationship?
- Give you something to do together?

Remember the greatest gift is the giving of yourself. The additional physical gifts you give highlight the fact that you see your grandchild as special and worthy of your time, attention, and resources.

Reading to a child is another great way to spend focused time. Sitting down and reading with your grandchild will help you open up their minds to new and exciting ideas.

> *If you see a book, a rocking chair, and a grandchild in the same room, don't pass up a chance to read aloud. Instill in your grandchild a love of reading. It's one of the greatest gifts you can give.*
> —Barbara Bush

Unhurried time spent reading with your grandchild is a wonderful way to communicate that they are special. Grandparents are usually not as busy as parents and can find time to pick up a book and read to children. When you read to your grandchild, let me encourage you to:

- Select age-appropriate books that will keep their interest.

- Find a comfortable place to snuggle up and to let their imagination grow.

- Read with feeling and expression to help children stay interested and experience fuller emotions.

- Read some books that can help them deal with real-life challenges.

- Remember that the goal is to spend quality time, so if they lose interest, feel free to move on to something else or another book.

Overall, grandparents generally have the gift of presence. They show up without a busy agenda of things they need to get done, people to meet, or places they need to go. They have time to spend just hanging out.

A grandparent will help you with your buttons, your zippers,
and your shoelaces and not be in a hurry for you to grow up.
—Erma Bombeck (American Humorist 1927-1996)

Grandparenting from a long distance is a challenging reality for many. Today, a lot of grandparents have grandchildren living far away in other cities and sometimes even other countries. Keeping in touch is hard for those doing long-distance grandparenting. We have established the fact that grandparents are needed and your role is important, but how can it be done from a distance? Can you still develop a close relationship with your grandchildren? It will not be as easy, but with creativity and modern technology, it is definitely possible.

Grandparenting from a distance can even have some advantages. For example, you are removed from the everyday stresses that affect your grandchild's family. I heard of a situation where a granddaughter lives with her parents in Australia, more than a twelve-hour flight away. The grandparents are only able to see her once a year, at best. Because of challenges in school, their grandchild needed to repeat the fifth grade. These grandparents were able to talk to their granddaughter over the phone and encourage her that repeating one grade in school was a very short time compared to the length of her whole life. She felt encouraged and later that summer she was able to come for a visit. The time with her grandparents gave her a change of pace from the big city. After that summer, her grades improved and she became one of the top students in her class. These grandparents knew they made a difference in their granddaughter's life, even though they didn't see her every day.

Using the telephone or talking via the computer is a great way to keep in touch from a distance. However, if your grandchild is not talkative, it can be a little more challenging. Here are some suggestions to help improve talk time with grandchildren via the telephone or computer:

1. Have a specific set of questions in mind as you begin your conversation.

2. If they answer with only yes or no responses, go on to follow-up questions.

3. Many follow-up questions start with what, where, who, and how. For example: What are you doing? Where did you go? Who went with you? How did you feel?

4. Be a sympathetic listener. Children and adults love to be listened to and understood. Your grandchildren are no different.

5. When grandchildren are young, it is just good for them to hear your voice. Don't be discouraged if they walk away from the phone after a while, but keep calling on a regular basis.

Another great way of keeping in touch includes the lost art of letter writing. Because fewer people send and receive mail these days, it can be very exciting for children to get a letter. Regardless of whether you communicate through the Internet, phone, or by slow mail, the important thing is that you stay in touch. By communicating regularly, you will be a part of your grandchild's life.

Loving grandchildren will be natural for most grandparents, but warm feelings are not enough. Developing a plan on how to show your love will require planning, effort, and persistence. Your grandchildren need you, and it is important to be needed.

The Sundial

The shadow by my finger cast,
Divides the future from the past,
Behind its unreturning line,
The vanished hour, no longer thine.
Before it lies the unknown hour,
In darkness and beyond thy power,
One hour alone is in thine hands:
The now on which the shadow stands.
—Wellesley College Sundial

Application points:

- What did you learn from this chapter that could improve your relationship with your grandchild?
- How can you take time to celebrate the wonderful season of grandparenting?
- What will you do first?
- For parents, thinking of the future, what do you hope for when you become a grandparent?

Chapter 29

· · · · · · · · · · · · · ·

A United Stand

· · · · · · · · · · · · · ·

When two people are one in their inmost hearts,
They shatter even the strength of iron or of bronze.
And when two people understand each other
in their inmost hearts,
Their words are sweet and strong,
like the fragrance of orchids.

—I Ching, *When Two People Are as One*

On a sports team, victory is achieved by working together and by learning from the coach. I have been blessed in my life by some great coaches on marriage and family. As I grew up, I could clearly see that my parents truly loved each other. This is the greatest gift parents can give their child. When kids know that Mom and Dad love each other, they feel secure. My parents did an excellent job raising my siblings and me, so we were able to learn about good parenting just by growing up. In my early twenties, I also sought other role models in order to learn from those who had strong families and mature children.

One of these role model couples was Tim and Joanie Thomas. Tim and Joanie stood out as an exceptional older couple that successfully raised eight children. I met them before I was married and took every opportunity possible to visit them and learn from their wisdom and experience. They opened up their home and allowed me to sit at their table and glean wisdom from what I heard and (mostly) from what I saw. I also took the opportunity after I was married to work alongside them for a few months in Hawaii at a local church. It was a rich time for my wife and me while we learned to raise our little one-year-old baby, Elizabeth. Their hospitality and daily life modeled a godly home that is still something I strive to emulate today. As our time was coming to an end, I asked Tim if he had any specific advice he would like to share with me before we left.

Tim said, "I saw a number of gifted teachers and leaders destroy their families by being unfaithful. Gifted teachers and preachers are not what this world needs most. People need to see that the family can work. Every person wants to feel loved. The first and most natural place they look for that love is in the family. Too many families have failed to provide environments for children to feel safe and loved, thus leaving a lot of lost and confused people out there. They are all looking for love, seeking leaders to show us how to find it. If you hope to mentor people to know God and enjoy a fulfilling life, let them watch your life. You can be a gifted teacher and pass on great wisdom, but if you can't show them that your family works, you will only be modeling hopelessness. If you, the teacher and mentor, can't make your family work, what hope is there for them? You could have knowledge to share, but your life will speak a hopeless message."

Tim's advice has rung in my ears for more than two decades. Loving, stable families are a fundamental need in every society in every corner of the globe. Fathers and mothers need to love one another and produce a home of safety for children to experience love. Without strong families, every society in this world will eventually fall. Tim's gem of wisdom shared that day in Hawaii has influenced the last twenty years of my life and blessed my family and me immensely.

> *There is nothing nobler or more admirable than when*
> *two people who see eye-to-eye keep house as man and wife,*
> *confounding their enemies and delighting their friends.*
> —Homer, *The Odyssey*

Intellectually believing that the world needs strong marriages is easy; becoming one of those strong marriages takes a lot of hard work. One of my favorite books on marriage is called *His Needs, Her Needs*. This book discusses the unique differences between the needs of men and women in a marriage. It also helps you define your top five needs in order of personal importance. Becoming aware of each other's needs and learning how to meet them can heal and transform most marriages.

Based on the author's research, the top ten felt needs for couples are: affection, sexual fulfillment, conversation, recreational companionship, honesty and openness, attractiveness of spouse, financial support, domestic support, family commitment, and admiration.1 These needs are common in marriage, but their order of importance is very different for women than it is for men. Some of the items that are most important for husbands may not even be listed on the wives' list. Take the time to fill out the list in Appendix E and talk about it with your spouse. Finding a mentor or taking a marriage class to help you work on your marriage is another way to make the most of this resource. United couples have the huge benefit of sharing the challenges and celebrating the victories of parenting.

> *What greater thing is there for two human souls, than to*
> *feel that they are joined for life—to strengthen each other*
> *in all labor, to rest on each other in all sorrow, to minister*
> *to each other in all pain, to be one with each other in silent*
> *unspeakable memories at the moment of the last parting?*
> —George Eliot, *Adam Bede*

I have heard people say that marriage is a 50/50 partnership. If both contribute their fifty percent, everything should be fair and the marriage will work. This sounds reasonable, but in reality this will fail every time. First, it will fail because marriage is not a business. It is much more complicated and much more important. Marriage is a relationship built on love, and love is giving by its very nature. In 50/50 relationships, people spend time adding up what the other is contributing, rather than focusing on their contribution.

When I try to serve my wife by doing fifty percent of the work around the house, this is what happens: I value my activities as important and calculate when I have given my share. My wife will also give a value level to the many activities she does and the way she contributes. The problems occur when we value our contributions with a higher ratio than our spouse would. For example, I took out the trash, which was a dirty, smelly job that forced me to go outside in the cold. I give it ten points as compared to my wife just doing the dishes after dinner, staying inside where it is comfortable. So doing dishes only counts as five points. But on the other hand, my wife is measuring her contribution based on time. Let's say the trash took two minutes and the dishes took thirty minutes. So in her calculations, I earned two points and she has now contributed thirty. At the end of the day, we both feel like we are being cheated and are contributing more than our fifty percent into the relationship. The concept of 50/50 just doesn't work. If you give one hundred percent into the marriage and remove your scorecard, you will have a chance to develop a good marriage.

Many people today complain, "Relationships are so hard. How can anyone expect to have a good marriage?" It is hard, and very, very, very important. I believe it is important enough for us to work at it. Here are a few principles that can help develop a strong marriage. Marriages get in trouble when a husband or wife's needs are not met. Most of us go into marriage expecting the other person to make us happy or at least not make us unhappy. Unfortunately in most cases, spouses seldom live up to expectations and end up hurting one another from time to time.

I remember my dad talking about marriage like a savings account in a bank. You make a deposit by creating good memories or by doing something to bless. When you hurt one another or disappoint, you are making a withdrawal. Some people with happy childhoods come into a marriage with a very full bank account; difficult childhoods usually result in low or emotionally empty bank accounts. A full relational bank account usually creates a happy couple. Low or negative balances in the relational bank account put the marriage at risk. People are much more complicated than bank accounts, but this is a simple analogy to help us think about how our actions affect our spouse.

Taking the time to identify what each other needs is a very important step in any healthy marriage. Some couples are afraid to do this because it might reveal some areas where they are not measuring up in their spouse's eyes. It might lead to a fight. Such an exercise will only reveal what is already there. If needs are not being met presently, then the passing of time will seldom make things better. In fact, consistently unmet needs in a marriage generally make a couple vulnerable to affairs.

A healthy, loving relationship between Mom and Dad is one of the most fundamental and important gifts that parents can give their child. To illustrate this point, I'll end this chapter with an Aesop Fable.

The Bundle of Sticks

A certain father had a family of sons who were constantly arguing among themselves. Nothing he said seemed to be getting through to them. So the father decided to teach them an object lesson.

One day when their fighting had reached such a point that all of them were moping about sadly, he sent them out to gather a bundle of sticks. He then divided up the sticks, tied them into bundles, and gave one to each son and asked them to try to break it. They used all their strength, but none were able to break their bundle. He then untied their bundles and gave them the sticks to break one by one. They had no trouble breaking all the sticks.

At this point he said, "My sons, don't you see that when you are in agreement and unity with each other, you are strong? When you are divided, you are weak and can be broken or defeated as easily as you broke the individual sticks."

Moral of the story: In unity is strength.

Application points:

- What did you learn from this chapter that you would like to implement?
- If you are married, what steps can you take today to improve your relationship with your spouse?
- What changes need to be made in order to keep your relationship growing in the future?

Chapter 30

· · · · · · · · · · · · · · · ·

Overcoming This Dark Age

· · · · · · · · · · · · · · · ·

The world will not be destroyed by those who do evil,
but by those who watch them without doing anything.

—Albert Einstein

When I was about twenty-four years old, I traveled to Guatemala where I spent three months living with friends. One day we decided to climb one of the active volcanoes near Guatemala City. The volcano was called Pacaya. It was a twin-cone volcano with one of the cones very active. The volcano became active back in 1965, and its smoking mouth was visible by day from the highway. Some days the eruptions only involved minor gaseous bursts with a few rocks. Other days it hurled bombs 7 miles (twelve kilometers) and caused evacuations of villages at its base.

On the day we climbed, one cone's peak was active and the other was not, which allowed us to climb to the top and look across to the active peak. I can still remember the smell of sulfur as we ascended close to the opening of the volcano. The ground was composed of loose ash and cinders. In addition to the sulfuric gasses emitting from small lava tubes, a dense cloud settled over us just before we reached the summit. The effect was very eerie as the volcano still actively spewed out small amounts of lava and pumice stones. Every eight minutes or so we heard a rumble as loud as a jet engine and felt the vibration of the lava and gases blasting out of the volcano. We couldn't see, but we could hear the sound of lava rocks falling near us. I loved the experience in spite of the danger.

Reaching the peak of the volcano's cone was a definite highlight, but the landscape surrounding the volcano also left a lasting impression in my mind. The fresh lava flows had destroyed every living thing within a half-mile radius of the volcano. The ground was blackened dirt, ash, and cinder with only a few charred tree trunks scattered across the landscape as reminders that life used to exist here. It resembled a scene from a prehistoric movie; I almost expected to see a dinosaur walk by or find one struggling for life in a tar pit.

Just as the lava destroyed all life on the hills surrounding the volcano, many bad influences flow like lava over children today. These destructive influences threaten to destroy all beauty, innocence, and life. Our child's world today is different from the world we grew up in. School, technology, and entertainment will have a huge influence on our child's development. Some of the influences of our modern age are good, but many are not. Media in all its forms seeks to have a great influence on our children. Unfortunately, the goal of most media is not to help our children become exceptionally moral and pure knights and princesses.

The way we can be sure that our children are not exposed to inappropriate media is to closely monitor what they see. This takes time, but our children need to learn as early as possible what is acceptable and what is forbidden. In our home, the main forms of information come in through books, music, and what became known as "screen time." "Screen time" means any activity that involves a flat screen with images moving across it (TV, computer, handheld electronic devices, video games, movies, etc.). Parents need to make it clear to their children that they have the right to monitor any form of media the kids choose to interact with. There is too much dangerous media out there for our children to deal with alone. That means you can and should check any electronic device like phones and computers from time to time.

Setting high standards for our children will be crucial in winning the battle against the negative effects of media. To do this, we need to be winning the battle ourselves. Media is an equally, and sometimes more, tempting form of escape for adults as it is for children. As our children reach adolescence, we should not be watching anything that we do not want them to watch as adults.

TV used to be dangerous in that it wasted time that could have been spent doing other activities. Today, TV is not just time consuming, it is increasingly violent, sexual, and perverted. Most parents wouldn't agree with the values taught by the majority of modern TV shows, but they regularly watch them and allow their children to do the same. Our values may be fixed, but our children's are still forming.

Another challenge of watching TV is the commercials. We can carefully select clean TV programs, thinking it is safe for the whole family to watch, and then a commercial comes on that exposes us to sexually suggestive images. Here are some suggestions that may help limit the negative effect TV can have on your family:

- Limit TV viewing to thirty or sixty minutes per day or set a maximum number of hours during the course of the week.

- Do not let your children channel surf. Only allow them to watch preselected programs on preselected stations.

- Record the programs ahead of time. This allows you to fast-forward the commercials, saving time and potentially negative information.

In spite of all our best efforts, our children will see things they shouldn't from time to time. When this happens, talk to them about why those things are not appropriate. You can also find out what your children are thinking and proactively prepare them for success by asking them to answer the following questions:

- When you're watching a movie or TV and people start taking off their clothes, what will you do?

- You are at a friend's house and watching a TV show that he says is really funny. Halfway through the show, you realize all the jokes are sexually suggestive and crude. What do you do?

- While listening to the radio with a friend, a song comes on that is full of swear words. What would you do?

- You are playing video games with a friend. He puts in a new game that is grossly violent. What do you do?

Helping kids think through appropriate responses to these situations greatly strengthens their chances of success.

Movies are another area that will test one's moral standards. In our home we initially screen out most nudity and bad language by keeping movies under a certain rating. However, the rating alone is not sufficient. Thankfully, checking websites that rates movies on violence, sexual content, language, and moral theme can help screen most movies more carefully. These sites give very detailed information on movie content. Our family has been able to avoid many movies because of these websites. We have been disappointed at times when we have been waiting for a movie sequel to come out and find that it is not as clean as the first one. In spite of the disappointment of not seeing it, I am thankful we checked and saved our family from being exposed to inappropriate material.

Pornography might be the biggest consistent danger all of our children face. It has easier access than alcohol, is as addictive as drugs, and destroys families every day. Teach your children that pornography will actually take away from the satisfaction they can experience in their marriages. It takes something that was created to be beautiful and intimate between a husband and wife and makes it dirty and shameful.

> *Like a muddied spring or a polluted well is a righteous man*
> *who gives way to the wicked.*
> —Proverbs 25:26

When you say the word pornography, your children may not know exactly what you mean. It is important to be clear without being too explicit. Pornography is any type of media that stimulates sexual desire. This involves magazines, books, Internet sites, and suggestive images in movies or on TV. Some music could also be considered pornographic in content if the lyrics are sexual in nature.

Make sure your children know the following:

- Pornography is dangerous; it can destroy your life and will hurt and/or destroy your future family and marriage.

- They are to be open and honest about what they watch, listen to, and entertain themselves with.

- All forms of media and communication should be above reproach and available for parents to see or listen to at any time.

Pornography quiz for parents: What would you do if...

- You see your son change the computer site or shut it down as soon as you enter the room?

- You find a pornographic picture under your son's bed? When you question him about it, he says he found it in the trash.

- You notice that your child has pictures on his phone that are sexually suggestive?

- Your daughter is reading a book that she says all her friends are reading? After reading a few pages, you realize the romantic content in the book is very sexually suggestive.

How you choose to deal with the above situations will differ greatly depending on your personal family values. However, the worst thing you can do is to ignore the situation. As a parent, keep your eyes wide open and protect your children from danger. Don't let the media or the computer come between you and your relationship with your child. We all need to fight for our kids' hearts, minds, souls, and bodies.

Remember that good kids can get pulled into bad situations. Keeping a vigilant eye on our child's friends and activities is important to keep them safe. Bad company does corrupt good character, as the following Aesop fable illustrates.

The Farmer and the Stork

A farmer placed nets on his newly sown plow lands and caught a number of cranes, which came to pick up his seed. With them he trapped a stork that had fractured his leg in the net and was earnestly beseeching the farmer to spare his life.

"Pray save me, Master," he said, "and let me go free this once. My broken limb should excite your pity. Besides, I am no crane, I am a stork, a bird of excellent character. See how I love and slave for my father and mother? Look, too, at my feathers—they are not the least like those of a crane."

The farmer laughed aloud and said, "It may be all as you say. I only know this: I have taken you with these robbers, the cranes, and you must die in their company."

Moral: you will be judged by the company you keep.

Application points:

- What did you learn from this chapter about the moral dangers facing your child?
- What can you proactively do to help your child grow up safe in today's world?
- What would be a first step in this process?

Chapter 31

. . . .

Love Makes the World Go Round

. . . .

All you need is love, all you need is love,
All you need is love, love, love is all you need.
—The Beatles, *All You Need Is Love*

The Beatles may not have had a perfect view of what true love really looked like, but they did a good job of emphasizing its importance. As we come to the final chapter of this book, let's take the perspective of one looking back over one's life. What will cause us to say that our life was well-spent, full, and rich? Older people have fewer activities on their calendars, fewer people fighting for their time, and fewer deadlines to meet. What they do have is time to reflect on their lives and remember. Hopefully they will have many good memories to think back on, memories of time well spent with family and friends.

I want to be a person who has a lot of good memories to look back on when I am old. In relationship to my children, now is the time for me to make those memories. Some may ask, how do you guarantee that you will have good memories to look back on? Can memories be planned? Can we schedule them, or do they just happen? The other morning, I was walking outside to throw the football with my eleven-year-old son, Adam. He is the baby of the family. He is almost entering adolescence, and Carolyn and I are seeing how quickly this season of parenting young children is coming to an end. As I walked to the area where we were going to play catch, I stopped to smell a flower growing on a shrub. My son turned around, walked back, and did the same. This was a fresh reminder that our kids watch everything we do. It also reminded me that many memories are made on the way to something else. The journey can create as many memories as the destinations. I am also reminded that many of the best things in life don't require money. Time and attention is the currency kids need the most from parents; the future will be here before we know it, and our children will be grown.

In this final chapter, I want to emphasize again the importance of helping our children feel our love. Regardless of what your individual child's love language is, all children have one overlapping need: they desire time with their parents. They want to be listened to and encouraged. One of the most natural times for this is at the end of the day. The final words you speak to your child before they fall asleep will have a deep psychological effect on their development. The last words of the day should be the best words. These words that a child hears before drifting off to sleep have a powerful impact on their hearts and minds. These words build their character and worldview. At the close of the day, our children shift from the activities of study or play and they become still. The hustle and bustle of daily activities slowly fades until our children have a time of silent reflection before slipping into unconscious slumber. This time can be a lonely point of separation from the security of siblings and parents. This is when children crave comfort, verbal encouragement, and kindness. If the last words heard before slipping off to sleep sting of failure, not measuring up, or harshness, then it stands to reason that anxiety could fill their subconscious hours of the night. Parents should avoid being harsh or critical at the closing of the day. Instead, we can comfort, encourage, and love.

Children will eventually outgrow the need for the support parents give; however, they slowly, if ever, outgrow the desire for good-night blessings. My own kids are used to me coming in, praying for them, and telling them I love them at the close of every day. Even my twenty-year-old daughter still enjoys this nighttime ritual when she is home on summer breaks from college.

Giving our kids a nighttime blessing is very important, but it is not always easy. Let's be realistic about the challenges. Experience has taught me that when my children go to bed, I am tired and worn out from a full day. My wife and I may be looking forward to some adult time with each other. We are ready to be finished with taking care of our children's needs, regardless of how much we love them. Nighttime is also a time when our children may refuse to obey us in going to bed, asking for one more drink of water or complaining of hunger pains as if they are starving. In these cases, it is still appropriate to maintain strong discipline and require full obedience. Once obedience is achieved, bedtime rituals can become a sweet time of connecting with our children. I remember reading many stories to our children when they were small. This ritual stopped as they began reading faster than me. After a long workday, they would often accuse me of skipping words, which revealed my tiredness and impatience. In spite of my occasional falling asleep in the middle of reading a page or my skipping words, the season of reading to my children before tucking them into bed created some very fond memories.

Many children, including my own, go through some anxiety related to bedtime rituals. Some of the stages in our home were more challenging than others. For example, Elizabeth, our oldest, liked to leave her bed at age four and join us in ours. She also wanted to see my face. Even when it was dark and she could see very little, the fact that my face was turned toward her gave her comfort. Our last child, Adam, would often call out in the darkness of his room, "Mama, Baba." We would answer, "Yes, Adam," and he would reply with, "Never mind." We knew he just wanted to hear our voices and know that we were near. He also went through a stage where he didn't want to be the last to fall asleep and nightly asked if we were planning on staying up for a while. These two behaviors were easier to deal with than his older brother's. During one vacation when Timothy was about eight years old, he would lie in his bed and start to think of friends far away. He would miss them so much that he would start crying, and if it continued too long, he would get himself so worked up he would vomit. That wasn't fun. Thankfully, that stage didn't last long. In spite of these few challenges, bedtime rituals created many positive memories in our home.

Wise parents will take advantage of the nighttime ritual in order to build confidence and character into their child. Bedtime is the golden moment for shaping a child's emotional security and confidence in life. Punishment should not be postponed until the end of the day. The last words of the day are most likely to be impressed deeply into the child's mind and heart. The last words a child hears at the end of the day should be words that we want them to think back on with fond memories as they grow older.

All parents make mistake and there is no magical formula for producing perfect kids. What is true is that love will make all the difference in raising healthy children. The desire to be loved is built-in; children are born needing and desiring love. Mother Teresa once said, "The hunger for love is much more difficult to remove than the hunger for bread." I want to take every chance I get to tell my children that I love them. I want to heed the advice of eight year old Jessica, who said, "You really shouldn't say 'I love you' unless you mean it. But if you mean it, you should say it a lot. People forget." Our knights and princesses need to hear how much they are loved. Let me close with two concepts of love.

When you love somebody, your eyelashes go up and down and little stars come out of you.
—Karen (Age 7)

Love is patient, love is kind. It does not envy, it does not boast, it is not proud. It does not dishonor others, it is not self-seeking, it is not easily angered, it keeps no record of wrongs. Love does not delight in evil but rejoices with the truth. It always protects, always trusts, always hopes, always perseveres.
—I Corinthians 13:4-7

I don't know how to shoot loving stars out of my eyelashes but if we follow the advice of I Corinthians maybe that is what our kids will see.

Enjoy raising your knight or princess!

Application points:
- What did you learn from this chapter that you would like to implement?
- What nighttime routine would you like to establish with your child?
- In what new ways can you communicate your love to your child?
- God is the greatest source of wisdom and love available to us as parents. If you don't already have a relationship with God through Jesus Christ, go to Appendix F to learn more.

APPENDIX A

Make a list of your positive and negative childhood experiences. Next to the positive and negative experiences, rate them on a scale of 1–10. One represents your worst experience, and ten your best.

Chart of Childhood Experiences

Describe your experience	Circle appropriate #	Current effect
	1 2 3 4 5 6 7 8 9 10	
	1 2 3 4 5 6 7 8 9 10	
	1 2 3 4 5 6 7 8 9 10	
	1 2 3 4 5 6 7 8 9 10	
	1 2 3 4 5 6 7 8 9 10	
	1 2 3 4 5 6 7 8 9 10	
	1 2 3 4 5 6 7 8 9 10	
	1 2 3 4 5 6 7 8 9 10	
	1 2 3 4 5 6 7 8 9 10	
	1 2 3 4 5 6 7 8 9 10	

APPENDIX B

Activity 1
First, list some families that you admire.

Then pick the best part of each example and list them.

After each point on your list, answer the following:

What resources, activities, and priorities would it take for this practice to become a pattern in our family?

Discuss what you feel is required to maintain your description of a good family (internal/external factors, family rules, external activities, clubs, church youth groups, etc.).

Activity 2
Work together to create a family mission statement.
Find step-by-step help at: http://simplemom.net/back-to-the-basics-create-a-family-mission-statement/.

Activity 3
Create some SMART goals to help you become the family you hope to be. A smart goal is: Specific, Measurable, Attainable, Realistic, Timely.

For more information or help in understanding how to create a SMART goal, go to www.summituniversitymedia.com.

APPENDIX C

Here are four basic steps in training your child to ask for forgiveness.

1. Acknowledge that you have done something that wronged them: "I was wrong," or "It was wrong for me to..."

2. Identify the specific action or attitude that was wrong: "What I did was selfish," or "What I did was dishonest."

3. Be specific of the wrong action or attitude: "I shouldn't have lost my temper and shouted. Next time I need to discipline you, I will do it without shouting."

4. Ask for forgiveness: "Will you forgive me?"

Most children will verbally forgive unless the behavior is a pattern and they do not believe you are sincere in your resolve to change. Regardless of your child's response, you have modeled asking forgiveness and turned a bad situation into a training opportunity.

APPENDIX D

Action Steps for Grandparents — Begin by answering the following questions:

What role do you want to have in your grandchild's life?

What traditions, stories, and values would you like to pass on to your grandchild?

What obstacles will you face in reaching your goal? For example: distance, personal time, resistance from parent, etc.

What does this new family feel they need?

What relationship do you need to develop, maintain, or repair with your child and their spouse to be welcomed into your grandchild's life in the way you desire?

The follow-through action points:

- Make a plan.
- Implement the plan.
- Evaluate the success.
- Make adjustments and keep at it.

Remember, ninety percent of success is just showing up.

For more grandparent ideas, go to: http://grandparents.about.com/od/games/Games_for_Grandparents_to_Play_With_Grandchildren.htm

APPENDIX E

Rank the following needs in order of importance to you personally. On a scale of 1–10, rank the following needs in the order that you feel are most important to your spouse, number one representing the most important and number ten the least. Cross out any needs that you do not feel apply to you. Feel free to fill in your own unique needs if they are not listed.

Your Needs	**NEEDS**	Your Opinion of Your Spouse's Needs
	Affection	
	Sexual Fulfillment	
	Conversation	
	Recreational Companionship	
	Honesty and Openness	
	Attractiveness of Spouse	
	Financial Support	
	Domestic Support	
	Family Commitment	
	Admiration	

APPENDIX F

How You Can Know God Personally

If you haven't known God personally, here are four principles that will help guide you into a relationship with Him:

1. God loves you and wants to have a relationship with you. "For God so loved the world that he gave his one and only Son, that whoever believes in him shall not perish but have eternal life" (John 3:16). God created all of us with a hope for life after death. God has made a way for us to spend eternity in a wonderful place with Him. "Now this is eternal life: that they may know you, the only true God, and Jesus Christ, whom you have sent" (John 17:3). He knows the details of your life and cares for you personally. So what prevents us from knowing God?

2. Man is sinful and separated from God, so we cannot know him personally or experience His love because of our sin. The Bible says, "All have sinned and fall short of the glory of God" (Romans 3:23). Visualize God in heaven and man on earth, with a great gulf separating the two. Man is continually trying to reach God and establish a personal relationship with Him through his own efforts, such as a good life, philosophy, or religion—but he inevitably fails. The Bible says, "The wages of sin is death [separation from God]" (Romans 6:23). The third principle explains the only way to bridge this separation.

3. Jesus Christ is God's only provision for man to come back into a right relationship with God. Jesus did this by dying. "God demonstrates his own love for us in this: While we were still sinners, Christ died for us" (Romans 5:8). Christ died and then rose again from the grave. "Christ died for our sins, just as the Scriptures said. He was buried, and he was raised from the dead on the third day, just as the Scriptures said. He was seen by Peter and then by the Twelve. After that, he was seen by more than

500 of his followers at one time..." (1 Corinthians 15:3–6, NLT). Jesus' message is clear. "Jesus answered, 'I am the way and the truth and the life. No one comes to the Father except through me'" (John 14:6).

4. Today you can accept Jesus Christ as Savior and Lord; then you can know God personally and experience His love. We become part of God's family when we surrender our life to Him. "As many as received him, to them He gave the right to become children of God, even to those who believe in His name" (John 1:12, NASB). You don't have to be perfect to become a Christ-follower.

Prayer is talking to God. Right now you can pray to God and become part of God's family.

Lord Jesus, I want to know you personally. Thank you for dying on the cross for my sins. I open the door of my life and receive you as my Savior and Lord. Thank you for forgiving me of my sins and giving me eternal life. Take control of my life. Make me the kind of person You want me to be.

If you want to begin a relationship with God through Jesus Christ, pray this prayer right now and Christ will forgive your sins and restore you into a new relationship with God.

If you prayed this prayer, congratulations and welcome to the family of God! Heaven is now rejoicing. Luke 15:7 says that when one sinner accepts Jesus Christ as his or her Savior, the angels rejoice. So there's a party going on in heaven right now because of your decision! You can know that you have eternal life. "God has given us eternal life, and this life is in his Son. He who has the Son has life; he who does not have the Son of God does not have life. I write these things to you who believe in the name of the Son of God so that you may know that you have eternal life" (1 John 5:11–13).

When you accepted Christ this is what happened:
1. Christ came into your life (Colossians 1:27).
2. Your sins were forgiven (Colossians 1:14).
3. You became a child of God (John 1:12).
4. You received eternal life (John 5:24).
5. You began the great adventure for which God created you (John 10:10; 2 Corinthians 5:17; and 1 Thessalonians 5:18).

In order to more fully understand your new relationship with God, let me encourage you to: (1) Pray to Him daily, just as you would talk to a good friend. (2) Read the Bible so that you can learn more about His love. (3) Find a good church with other Christians that are also praying and reading God's word.

Again, welcome to the family of God!

Endnotes

Section II. Princess in Training

Chapter 2. A Princess Sets the Standard
1. From an interview by Martin Bashir on the BBC's Panorama, broadcast 20 November 1995.

Chapter 5. A Princess Enjoys Beauty
1. Mabel Hale, *Beautiful Girlhood* (Eugene, Oregon: Great Expectations Book Company, 1993), p. 42.
2. *Ibid.*, pp. 43-44.

Chapter 7. A Princess Needs Her Dad
1. Meg Meeker, *Strong Fathers, Strong Daughters: 10 Secrets Every Father Should Know* (Ballantine Books: New York, 2006), p. 8.
2. *Ibid.*, pp. 26–28.

Section III. Knight in Training

Chapter 8. Boys Becoming Knights
1. Alfred Tennyson, *Idylls of the King* (Penguin: London, 2004), p. 39.

Chapter 10. Becoming a Knight
1. "The Knights Templar: In Praise of the New Knighthood." www.templarhistory.com. Accessed 13 June 2011.

Chapter 11. Forming a Knight's Vision
1. Alfred Tennyson, *Sir Galahad*, 1842. http://en.wikipedia.org/wiki/Sir_Galahad_(poem). Accessed 30 November 2012.

Section IV. Strong Foundations

Chapter 14. Barriers to Raising Knights and Princesses
1. For a list of six obstacles to successful parenting, read: Reb Bradley, *Child Training Tips: What I Wish I Knew When My Children Were Young* (Fair Oaks, California: Family Ministries Publishing, 1998), p.15.
2. Printed in the Journal of the American Institute of Criminal Law and Criminality 18, no. 1 (May 1927) as written in the Minnesota Crime Commission report of 1926, which was commissioned by then Governor Theodore Christianson.
3. Wikipedia, "John Stephen Akhwari." http://en.wikipedia.org/wiki/John_Stephen_Akhwari. Accessed 30 November 2012.

Chapter 16. Child Training in the Home
1. Mary Rita Schilke Sill, "When You Thought I Wasn't Looking," (Granger, Indiana: Mary Rita Schilke Sill, 1980).

Chapter 17. Training through Role-Play (Good, Better, Best)
1. Adapted, with additions, from Reb Bradley, *Child Training Tips: What I Wish I Knew When My Children Were Young* (Fair Oaks, California: Family Ministries Publishing, 1998), pp. 142-143.

Chapter 18. Intimidated Parents and Child-Run Homes
1. Edward, Duke of Windsor, *Look*, 5 March 1957.
2. Adapted, with additions, from Reb Bradley, *Child Training Tips: What I Wish I Knew When My Children Were Young* (Fair Oaks, California: Family Ministries Publishing, 1998), p. 42.
3. *Ibid.*, p. 29.

Chapter 19. Regaining Authority
1. T. H. Palmer, *Teacher's Manual* (Boston: Marsh, Capen, Lyon, and Webb Education Press, 1840), p. 223.
2. Adapted, with additions, from Reb Bradley, *Child Training Tips: What I Wish I Knew When My Children Were Young* (Fair Oaks, California: Family Ministries Publishing, 1998).

3. Lindsey O'Conner, *Moms Who Changed the World* (Eugene, Oregon: Harvest House, 1999), p. 65.

Section V. Behavioral Basics

Chapter 20. Do Not Exasperate Your Children
1. For a much larger list of exasperating behaviors, read: Reb Bradley, *Child Training Tips: What I Wish I Knew When My Children Were Young* (Fair Oaks, California: Family Ministries Publishing, 1998), p. 147.
2. Robert Fulghum, All I Really Needed to Know I Learned in Kindergarten.http://www.goodreads.com/author/quotes/19630. Robert_Fulghum. Accessed 30 November 2012.

Chapter 21. Training in Wisdom
1. Adapted, with additions, from Reb Bradley, *Child Training Tips: What I Wish I Knew When My Children Were Young* (Fair Oaks, California: Family Ministries Publishing, 1998), p. 48.
2. Rudyard Kipling, "IF," (*A Choice of Kipling's Verse*, 1943).

Chapter 23. Overcoming Self-Indulgence and Excuses Kids Make
1. Adapted from Reb Bradley, *Child Training Tips: What I Wish I Knew When My Children Were Young* (Fair Oaks, California: Family Ministries Publishing, 1998), pp. 87–89.
2. *Ibid.*, pp. 107–12.

Chapter 24. Training a Child's Appetite
1. Adapted, with additions, from Reb Bradley, *Child Training Tips: What I Wish I Knew When My Children Were Young* (Fair Oaks, California: Family Ministries Publishing, 1998), p. 145.

Chapter 25. Dealing with Rebellion
1. Winston Churchill, Address at Harrow School, 29 October 1941. Cited in John Bartlett, *Bartlett's Familiar Quotations*, 16th ed. (Boston: Little, Brown and Company, 1992), p. 621.

2. Adapted from Reb Bradley, *Child Training Tips: What I Wish I Knew When My Children Were Young* (Fair Oaks, California: Family Ministries Publishing, 1998), p. 76.

3. *Ibid.*, pp. 78–79.

4. H. C. Trumbull, *Hints on Child Training* (Philadelphia: John C. Wattles & Co., 1890), p. 129.

5. Adapted from Reb Bradley, *Child Training Tips: What I Wish I Knew When My Children Were Young* (Fair Oaks, California: Family Ministries Publishing, 1998), p. 85.

Section VI. It Takes a Village

Chapter 27. The Grandparents' Blessings
1. Margaret Mary Kimmel and Mark Collins, The Wonder of It All, p. 7. http://www.fredrogerscenter.org/media/site_images/Kimmel_and_Collins-pdf_of_pub_version-10-15-08.pdf. Accessed 26 October 2012.

Chapter 29. A United Stand
1. Willard F. Harley Jr., *His Needs, Her Needs* (Grand Rapids: Fleming H. Revel, 2011), p. 18.

Coming Soon

The stories of Kleophis and Anna come to life in two beautifully illustrated children's books: *Knights of the Eastern Watchtower* and *The Lost Princess*. Watch for availability at SummitUniversityMedia.com.